SAINT GERMAIN

Mystery
of the
Violet Flame

GW00655892

ELIZABETH CLARE PROPHET

SUMMIT UNIVERSITY 🦢 PRESS®
Gardiner, Montana

SAINT GERMAIN
Mystery of the Violet Flame
Elizabeth Clare Prophet
Copyright © 2021 The Summit Lighthouse, Inc.
All rights reserved.

For information: The Summit Lighthouse,
63 Summit Way, Gardiner, MT 59030 USA
1-800-245-5445 / 406-848-9500
TSLinfo@TSL.org
www.SummitLighthouse.org

Library of Congress Control Number: 2021940770
ISBN: 978-1-60988-365-2
ISBN: 978-1-60988-366-9 (eBook)

Summit University Press®

Summit University Press, 🜍, Keepers of the Flame, and The Summit Lighthouse are trademarks registered in the U.S. Patent and Trademark Office and in other countries. All rights reserved.

24   23   22   21   1   2   3   4

CONTENTS

INTRODUCTION

We are in a moment of the greatest revolution ever known. It doesn't take great perception to read the handwriting upon the wall of events in this and every nation. We read the news. We look here. We look there. And there are days we would rather not look.

There is a very deep fear—a fear of something that the soul knows at subconscious levels but is not able to face in the conscious mind. It is a fear of coming events. We fear to bring forth from the dimness of an ancient memory the soul awareness of a shocking past—and an even more shocking future. And because we don't allow it to surface, we have a nation of insomnia, emotional and mental disorders, heart failure, and terminal disease.

We all sense an impending something. People are in a state of panic at subconscious levels. And that panic outpictures in wars across the face of the earth as the valve of the pressure cooker of the subconscious is opened just a little bit. Out it comes—like Pandora's box. The failure to resolve the inner components of being.

Inharmony within results in outer chaos. And yet we say, "What can *I* do? There's no point looking beyond my personal interests because I can't do anything anyway."

We think of the time before lightning was harnessed into electricity or before Einstein split the atom and gave us the formula $E=mc^2$. We say those were the dark ages. But today we know no more about the imprisoned lightning of God within us than was known centuries ago about the most basic physical forces.

It is so near and so close. Yet we are on the brink of self-destruction because we have allowed ourselves to say that God is past or future or in here or over there—but never close enough to be that practical application for the healing of our souls.

There are spiritual forces within us—within every single atom and cell, within the fire of our heart. If we would discover what these forces are, we would know how the fervent, white-hot heat of meditative love can burst that atom of Self and release the energy that has framed the worlds, that has created and uncreated the Void. It can begin a revolution of light. And it can make the imminent Aquarian age truly an era of peace and enlightenment.

The cycles of God Self-awareness move in two-thousand-year periods. In each two-thousand-year cycle, there's a dawning of a great light. In the age of Aries, the Judaic tradition taught us to understand God the Father, the personal God individualized in what Moses experienced as the I AM THAT I AM.

The next two-thousand-year period, marked by the coming of the avatar Jesus Christ, was the Piscean dispensation, which was intended to give us the understanding of God as Son. And so through reincarnation, lifetime after lifetime we were intended to put on the consciousness of God the Father and God the Son.

Now as we feel the winds of the Aquarian age, we find the energy of the Holy Spirit upon us in many ways: new sounds, new rhythms, new science, new technology—and, above all, a new freedom.

The Aquarian age is the moment of understanding energy and its conquest in time and space through the perfect polarity of the masculine and feminine principles of the universe—Spirit ("heaven") / Matter ("earth"). The "cloven tongues" of fire that sat upon each of the disciples on the day of Pentecost are these "twin flames" of the Father-Mother God that give to us the impact, the energy, the control of creative flow.

This descent of the Holy Spirit is a tremendous force. It is intense love. And this love-action is transmutative—that is, when this energy flows through us it is able to re-create us after the image of the Real Self.

Just as Jesus stood as the open door to the attainment of the Christ consciousness in the two-thousand-year Piscean cycle, so the Aquarian master Saint Germain comes today to initiate us on the path of soul liberation through the sacred fire of the Holy Spirit, that we call the violet flame.

SAINT GERMAIN: ALCHEMIST, ADEPT AND VISIONARY

Saint Germain lived to make us free. That, in a phrase, sums up Saint Germain's many incarnations. Although he has played many parts, in each life he has brought the Christ/Light in prophecy and the alchemy of freedom to liberate the people of earth.

He comes to the fore as Master of the Seventh Ray and Age. He comes to initiate us in the gift of *prophecy* and the gift of the *working of miracles*— that we might foresee by the Spirit of the prophets what is coming upon us and turn the tide by the miracle violet flame.

The Ascended Master Saint Germain

AN ANCIENT GOLDEN-AGE CIVILIZATION

More than fifty thousand years ago, a golden-age civilization thrived in a fertile country with a semitropical climate where the Sahara Desert now is. It was filled with great peace, happiness and prosperity and ruled with supreme justice and wisdom by this very Saint Germain.

The majority of his subjects retained full, conscious use of the wisdom and power of God. They possessed abilities that today would seem superhuman or miraculous. They knew they were extensions of the Central Sun—lifestreams issuing from the Great Hub of the Spirit-Matter cosmos.

For their wise ruler had charted for them on a great mural in the center of the capital city, "the City of the Sun," their cosmic history—that they should not forget the Source whence they had come nor their reason for being: to become sun centers in this distant galaxy they now called home, extensions of the Law of the One. For they were part of an expanding universe. And their sense of co-measurement with the One sustained an ever-present cognition of the I AM THAT I AM.

Saint Germain was a master of the ancient wisdom and of the knowledge of the Matter spheres. He ruled by Light every area of life; his empire reached a height of beauty, symmetry and perfection unexceeded in the physical octave. Truly the heavenly patterns were outpictured in the crystal chalice of the earth. And elemental life served to maintain the purity of the Matter quadrants.

The people regarded their hierarch as the highest expression of God whom they desired to emulate, and great was their love for his presence. He was the embodiment of the archetype of universal Christhood for that dispensation—to whom they could look as the standard for their own emerging Godhood.

Guy W. Ballard, under the pen name of Godfré Ray King, recounted in *Unveiled Mysteries* a soul journey in which Saint Germain conducted him through the akashic record of this civilization and its decline.[1]

Saint Germain explained to him that "as in all ages past, there was a portion of the people who became more interested in the temporary pleasures of the senses than in the larger creative plan of the Great God Self. This caused them to lose consciousness of the God-power throughout the land until it remained active in little more than the [capital] city itself. . . . Those governing realized they must withdraw and let the people learn, through hard experience, that all their happiness and good came from the adoration to the God within, and they must come back into the light if they were to be happy."

Thus, the ruler was instructed by a cosmic council that he must withdraw from his empire and his beloved people; henceforth their karma would be their Guru and Lawgiver, and free will would determine what, if any, of his legacy of light they would retain.

According to plan, the king held a great banquet in the Jeweled Room of his palace, with his councillors and public servants in attendance. Following the dinner, which had been entirely precipitated, a crystal goblet filled with "pure electronic essence" appeared to the right of each of the 576 guests. It was the communion cup of Saint Germain, who, with the mantle and scepter of the ancient priest/ kings, gave of his own light essence to those who had faithfully served the realm to the glory of God.

As they drank to the "Flame of the Most High

Living One," they knew they could never completely forget the divine spark of the inner God Self. This soul-protection, afforded them through the ever-grateful heart of Saint Germain, would be sustained throughout the centuries until once again they should find themselves in a civilization where the cosmic cycles had turned and they would be given the full knowledge to pursue the Divine Union—this time nevermore to go out from the Golden City of the Sun.

Now a Cosmic Master from out the Great Silence spoke. His message was broadcast from the banquet hall throughout the realm. The resplendent being, who identified himself solely by the word *Victory* written upon his brow, brought warning of crisis to come, rebuked the people for their ingratitude to and neglect of their Great God Source, and reminded them of the ancient command to obey the Law of the One—Love. Then he gave them the following prophecy of their karma:

"A visiting prince approaches your borders. He will enter this city seeking the daughter of your king. You will come under the rule of this prince but the recognition of your mistake will be futile. Nothing can avail, for the royal family will be drawn into the protection and care of those whose power and authority are of God, and against whom no human desire can ever prevail. These are the great ascended masters of light from the golden etheric city over this land. Here your ruler and his beloved children will abide for a cycle of time."

The king and his children withdrew seven days later. The prince arrived the next day and took over without opposition.

As we study the history of Saint Germain's lifestream we shall see that time and time again the master and his way of God-mastery have been rejected by the very ones he sought to help; notwithstanding the fact that his gifts of light, life and love—fruits of his adeptship freely given—his alchemical feats, elixir of youth, inventions and prognostications have been readily received.

The goal of his embodiments extending from the golden-age civilization of the Sahara to the final hour of his life as Francis Bacon was always to liberate the children of the light, especially those who in their carelessness in handling fiery principles of the Law had been left to their own karmic devices—in whose vices they were often bound. His aim was to see the fulfillment of his prayer offered at the final banquet of his reign:

> If they must have the experience that consumes and burns away the dross and clouds of the outer self, then do Thou sustain and at last bring them forth in Thy Eternal Perfection. I call unto Thee, Thou Creator of the Universe—Thou Supreme Omnipotent God.

THE VIOLET FLAME TEMPLE ON ATLANTIS

As the high priest of the Violet Flame Temple on the mainland of Atlantis thirteen thousand years ago, Saint Germain sustained by his invocations and his causal body a pillar of fire, a fountain of violet singing flame, which magnetized people from near and far to be set free from every binding condition of body, mind and soul. This they achieved by self-effort through the offering of invocations and the practice of seventh-ray rituals to the sacred fire.

An intricately carved marble circular railing enclosed the shrine where suppliants knelt in adoration of the God flame—visible to some as a physical violet flame, to others as an "ultraviolet" light and to others not at all, though the powerful healing vibrations were undeniable.

The temple was built of magnificent marble ranging in hue from brilliant white, shot through with violet and purple veins, to deeper shades of the seventh-ray spectrum. The central core of the temple was a large circular hall lined in ice-violet marble set upon a rich purpled marble floor. Three stories in height, it was situated midst a complex of adjacent areas for worship and the various functions of priests and priestesses who ministered unto the flame and mediated its voice of light and prophecy unto the people. Those who officiated at this altar were schooled in the universal priesthood of the Order of Melchizedek at Archangel Zadkiel's retreat, the Temple of Purification, in the locale of the West Indies.

Through the heights and depths of the ages that have ensued, Saint Germain has ingeniously used the seventh-ray momentum of his causal body to secure freedom for keepers of the flame who have kept alive "coals" from the violet-flame altar of his Atlantean temple. He has extolled and exemplified freedom of the mind and spirit. Endowing the four sacred freedoms with an identity of their own, he has championed our freedom from state interference, kangaroo courts, or popular ridicule in matters ranging from scientific investigation to the healing arts to the spiritual quest.

Standing on a platform of basic human rights for a responsible, reasoning public educated in the principles of liberty and equal opportunity for all, he has ever taught us to espouse our inalienable divine right to live life according to our highest conception of God. For the master has said that no right, however simple or basic, can long be secure without the underpinning of the spiritual graces and the Divine Law that instills a compassionate righteousness in the exercise thereof.

THE PROPHET SAMUEL

Returning to the scene of the karma of his people as Samuel, prophet of the LORD and judge of the twelve tribes of Israel (c. 1050 B.C.), Saint Germain was the messenger of God's liberation of the seed of Abraham from bondage to the corrupt priests, the sons of Eli, and from the Philistines by whom they had been defeated. Bearing in his

Samuel Anointing David, by Antonio González Velázquez

When the disobedient King Saul rejected the word of the LORD and the LORD rejected him from being king, "for rebellion is as the sin of witchcraft, and stubbornness is as iniquity and idolatry," the LORD sent Samuel to the house of Jesse in Bethlehem to anoint the shepherd boy David, youngest of Jesse's sons, to be king of Israel.   (I Samuel 15, 16)

heart the special sign of the blue rose of Sirius, Samuel delivered to the recalcitrant Israelites a prophecy parallel to his twentieth-century discourses —both inextricably linked with God's covenants concerning karma, free will and grace:

"If ye do return unto the LORD with all your hearts, then put away the strange gods and Ashtaroth from among you, and prepare your hearts unto the LORD and serve him only: and he will deliver you out of the hand of the Philistines." Later, when King Saul disobeyed God, Samuel freed the people from his tyranny by anointing David king.

We see, then, in each of Saint Germain's embodiments that there is present the quality of alchemy —a conveyance of godly power. So ordained as the instrument of the LORD, Samuel transferred His sacred fire in the anointing of David and just as scientifically withdrew it from King Saul when the LORD rejected him from being king over Israel.

SAINT JOSEPH

True to the thread of prophecy that runs throughout his lifetimes, Saint Germain was Saint Joseph of the lineage of King David, son of Jesse, chosen vessel of the Holy Ghost, father of Jesus in fulfillment of the word of the LORD to Isaiah—"There shall come forth a rod out of the stem of Jesse, and a Branch shall grow out of his roots."[2]

The Vision of St. Joseph, Philippe de Champaigne

"Behold, the angel of the Lord appeareth to Joseph in a dream, saying, Arise, and take the young child and his mother, and flee into Egypt, and be thou there until I bring thee word: for Herod will seek the young child to destroy him. When he arose, he took the young child and his mother by night, and departed into Egypt."
(Matthew 2:13, 14)

SAINT ALBAN, FIRST BRITISH MARTYR

This unmistakable sign of the seventh-ray adept, often in humble garb, was also present as the Holy Spirit's power of the conversion of souls and the control of natural forces in his life as the third-century Saint Alban, first martyr of the British Isles.

Alban was a Roman soldier who hid a fugitive priest, was converted by him, then sentenced to death for disguising himself as the priest and allowing him to escape. A great multitude gathered to witness his execution—too many to pass over the narrow bridge that must be crossed. Alban prayed and the river parted—whereupon his executioner, being converted, begged to die in Alban's place. His request was denied and he was beheaded that day alongside the saint.

SHAPING THE PHILOSOPHY OF WESTERN CIVILIZATION

But Saint Germain was not always to be counted in the ranks of the Church. He fought tyranny wherever he found it, including in false Christian

St. Alban, Evesham All Saints' Church, Lincoln, UK

Britain's first martyr, Alban, has been revered by the people of the Isles since his death in A.D. 303. As the Reverend Alban Butler writes in his *Lives of the Fathers, Martyrs and other Principal Saints,* "Our island for many ages had recourse to St. Alban as its glorious protomartyr and powerful patron with God, and acknowledged many great favours received from God, through his intercession."

doctrine. As the master teacher behind the Neoplatonists, Saint Germain was the inner inspiration of the Greek philosopher Proclus (c. A.D. 410–485). He revealed his pupil's previous life as a Pythagorean philosopher, also showing Proclus the sham of Constantine's Christianity and the worth of the path of individualism (leading to the individualization of the God flame), which Christians called "paganism."

As the highly honored head of Plato's Academy at Athens, Proclus based his philosophy upon the principle that there is only one true reality—the "One," which is God, or the Godhead, the final goal of all life's efforts. The philosopher said, "Beyond all bodies is the essence of soul, and beyond all souls the intellectual nature, and beyond all intellectual existences the One."[3] Throughout his incarnations Saint Germain demonstrated tremendous breadth of knowledge in the mind of God; not surprising was the range of his pupil's awareness. His writings extended to almost every department of learning.

Proclus acknowledged that his enlightenment and philosophy came from above—indeed he believed himself to be one through whom divine revelation reached mankind. "He did not appear to be without divine inspiration," his disciple Marinus wrote, "for he produced from his wise mouth words similar to the most thick-falling snow; so that his eyes emitted a bright radiance, and the rest of his countenance participated of divine illumination."[4]

Thus Saint Germain, white-robed, jeweled slippers and belt emitting star-fire from far-off worlds, was the mystery master smiling just beyond the veil —mirroring the imagings of his mind in the soul of the last of the great Neoplatonic philosophers.

MERLIN

Saint Germain was Merlin. The unforgettable, somehow irretrievable figure who haunts the mists of England, about to step forth at any moment to offer us a goblet of sparkling elixir. He the "old man" who knows the secrets of youth and alchemy, who charted the stars at Stonehenge, and moved a stone or two, so they say, by his magical powers— who would astonish no one if he suddenly appeared on a Broadway stage or in the forests of the Yellowstone or at one's side on any highway anywhere.

Merlin with the infant Arthur, by N. C. Wyeth

Merlin was King Arthur's guiding spirit even before his birth. The legends say that in exchange for arranging the union of Uther Pendragon and Ygerne of Cornwall, Merlin demanded that he should have the child that would be born, Arthur. Merlin caused the sword and the stone to appear in the churchyard of Canterbury Cathedral. By the trial of the sword—representing the power of the soul that is free from the bondage of attachment to things material symbolized by the stone and anvil—Arthur proved his kingship. Thereafter, Merlin remained at Arthur's side as counselor and friend.

For Saint Germain *is* Merlin. Merlin has never left us—his spirit charms the ages, makes us feel as rare and unique as his diamond and amethyst adornments. Merlin is the irreplaceable presence, a humming vortex about whose science and legends and fatal romance Western civilization has entwined itself.

It was the fifth century. Midst the chaos left by the slow death of the Roman Empire, a king arose to unite a land splintered by warring chieftains and riven by Saxon invaders. At his side was the old man himself—half Druid priest, half Christian saint—seer, magician, counselor, friend, who led the king through twelve battles to unite a kingdom and establish a window of peace.

At some point, the spirit of Merlin went through a catharsis. The scene was one of fierce battle, the legend says. As he witnessed the carnage, a madness came upon him—of seeing all at once past, present and future—so peculiar to the lineage of the prophets. He fled to the forest to live as a wild man, and one day as he sat under a tree, he began to utter prophecies concerning the future of Wales.

King Arthur receiving the sword Excalibur, by N. C. Wyeth

The young King Arthur once would have died by the sword of mighty Pellinore had not Merlin appeared and "cast an enchantment" upon the knight. It was because Arthur's sword was smitten in two during that fierce joust that Merlin and Arthur rode to the lake where they miraculously beheld rising from the water the arm of the Lady of the Lake holding the magnificent sword Excalibur.

"I was taken out of my true self," he said. "I was as a spirit and knew the history of people long past and could foretell the future. I knew then the secrets of nature, bird flight, star wanderings and the way fish glide."[5] Both his prophetic utterances and his "magical" powers served one end: the making of a united kingdom of the tribes of the old Britons. His pervasiveness is recalled in an early Celtic name for Britain, "Clas Myrddin," which means "Merlin's Enclosure."[6]

By advising and assisting Arthur in establishing his kingship, Merlin sought to make of Britain a fortress against ignorance and superstition where Christ achievement could flower and devotion to the One could prosper in the quest for the Holy Grail. His efforts on this soil were to bear fruit in the nineteenth century as the British Isles became the place where individual initiative and industry could thrive as never before in twelve thousand years.

But even as Camelot, the rose of England, budded and bloomed, nightshade was twining about its roots. Witchcraft, intrigue and treachery destroyed Camelot, not the love of Launcelot and Guinevere as Sir Thomas Malory's misogynistic depiction suggests. Alas, the myth he sowed has obscured the real culprits these long centuries.

It was the king's bastard son Modred by his half sister Margawse[7] who, with Morgana le Fay and a circle of like sorceresses and black knights, set out to steal the crown, imprison the queen, and destroy for a time the bonds of a love that such as these (of the left-handed path) had never known nor could —a reality all of their willing, warring and enchantments could not touch.

Thus it was with a heavy heart and the spirit of a prophet who has seen visions of tragedy and desolation, fleeting joys and the piercing anguish of karmic retribution endlessly outplayed, that Merlin entered the scene of his own denouement, to be tied up in spells of his own telling by silly, cunning Vivien —and sleep. Aye, to err is human but to pine for the twin flame that is not there is the lot of many an errant knight or king or lonely prophet who perhaps should have disappeared into the mists rather than suffer sad ignominy for his people.

ROGER BACON
AND THE DAWN OF SCIENCE

Some say he still sleeps, but they grossly underestimate the resilient spirit of the wise man. He returned in thirteenth-century England disguised as Roger Bacon (c. 1214–1294). Reenter Merlin—scientist, philosopher, monk, alchemist and prophet—to forward his mission of laying the scientific moorings for the age of Aquarius his soul should one day sponsor.

However, just as Saint Germain tells us today in his *Saint Germain On Alchemy* that "miracles" are wrought by the precise application of universal laws, so Roger Bacon meant his prophecies to demonstrate that flying machines and magical apparatus were products of the employment of natural law which men would figure out in time.

From whence did Bacon believe he derived his amazing awareness? "True knowledge stems not from the authority of others, nor from a blind allegiance to antiquated dogmas," he said. Two of his biographers write that he believed knowledge "is a

Roger Bacon, by Howard Pyle

The monk-scientist in his study, surrounded by the collected occult and scientific wisdom of the ages, from *The Key of Solomon*, which was supposed to contain the Hebrew kings' magic formulas, to the Persian physician Avicenna's *The Canon of Medicine*, to works on Greek Philosophy.

highly personal experience—a light that is communicated only to the innermost privacy of the individual through the impartial channels of all knowledge and of all thought."[8]

And so Bacon, who had been a lecturer at Oxford and the University of Paris, determined to separate himself and his thoughts from the posing and postulating residents of academe. He would seek and find his science in his religion. Entering the Franciscan Order of Friars Minor, he said, "I will conduct my experiments on the magnetic forces of the lodestone at the selfsame shrine where my fellow-scientist, St. Francis, performed his experiments on the magnetic forces of love."[9]

But the friar's scientific and philosophical world view, his bold attacks on the theologians of his day, and his study of alchemy, astrology and magic led to charges of "heresies and novelties," for which he was imprisoned in 1278 by his fellow Franciscans! They kept him in solitary confinement for fourteen years,[10] releasing him only shortly before his death. Although the clock of this life was run out, his body broken, he knew that his efforts would not be without impact on the future.

The following prophecy that he gave his students shows the grand and revolutionary ideals of the indomitable spirit of this living flame of freedom —the immortal spokesman for our scientific, religious and political liberties:

I believe that humanity shall accept as an axiom for its conduct the principle for which I have laid down my life—the right to investigate. It is the credo of free men— this opportunity to try, this privilege to err, this courage to experiment anew. We scientists of the human spirit shall experiment, experiment, ever experiment. Through centuries of trial and error, through agonies of research... let us experiment with laws and customs, with money systems and governments, until we chart the one true course— until we find the majesty of our proper orbit as the planets above have found theirs.... And then at last we shall move all together in the harmony of our spheres under the great impulse of a single creation—one unity, one system, one design.[11]

THE PROPHECY OF THE NEW WORLD

To establish this freedom upon earth, Saint Germain's lifestream took another turn—as Christopher Columbus (1451–1506). But over two centuries before Columbus sailed, Roger Bacon had set the stage for the voyage of the three ships and the discovery of the New World when he stated in his *Opus Majus* that "the sea between the end of Spain on the west and the beginning of India on the east is navigable in a very few days if the wind is favorable."[12]

Although the statement was incorrect in that the land to the west of Spain was not India, it was instrumental in Columbus' discovery. Cardinal Pierre d'Ailly copied it in his *Imago Mundi* without noting Bacon's authorship. Columbus read his work and quoted the passage in a 1498 letter to King Ferdinand and Queen Isabella, saying that his 1492 voyage had been inspired in part by this visionary statement.

Columbus believed that God had made him to be "the messenger of the new heaven and the new earth of which He spake in the Apocalypse of St. John, after having spoken of it by the mouth of Isaiah."[13]

His vision went back as far as ancient Israel, perhaps even further. For in discovering the New World, Columbus believed that he was the instrument whereby God would, as Isaiah recorded around 732 B.C., "recover the remnant of his people...and shall assemble the outcasts of Israel, and gather together the dispersed of Judah from the four corners of the earth."[14]

Twenty-two centuries passed before anything visible happened that seemed to be the fulfillment of this prophecy. But late in the fifteenth century, Christopher Columbus was quietly preparing to set the stage for the fulfillment of this prophecy, certain that he had been divinely selected for his mission. He studied the biblical prophets, writing passages relating to his mission in a book of his own making entitled *Las Proficias* or *The Prophecies*—in its complete form, *The Book of Prophecies concerning the Discovery of the Indies and the Recovery of Jerusalem.* Although the point is seldom stressed, it is a fact so rooted in history that even *Encyclopaedia Britannica* says unequivocally that, "Columbus discovered America by prophecy rather than by astronomy."[15]

Portrait of a Man, Said to Be Christopher Columbus,
by Sebastiano del Piombo

Columbus has been seen as a pivotal figure in history, the man who initiated the modern age. His discovery unified the world and set in motion the process of global integration. The discovery of the New World transformed the Old World, setting the stage for a new age.

"In the carrying out of this enterprise of the Indies," he wrote to King Ferdinand and Queen Isabella in 1502, "neither reason nor mathematics nor maps were any use to me: fully accomplished were the words of Isaiah." He was referring to Isaiah 11:10–12.

Thus we see that lifetime by lifetime, Saint Germain, whether his outer mind was continuously cognizant of it we know not, was re-creating that golden pathway to the Sun—a destiny come full circle to worship the God Presence and reestablish a lost golden age.

SIR FRANCIS BACON: SCIENTIST, STATESMAN, POET

As Francis Bacon (1561–1626), the greatest mind the West has ever produced, his manifold achievements in every field catapulted the world into a stage set for the children of Aquarius. In this life he was free to carry to its conclusion the work he had begun as Roger Bacon.

Scholars have noted the similarities between the thoughts of the two philosophers and even between Roger Bacon's *Opus Majus* and Francis Bacon's

"Could I but paint his mind," famed miniaturist Nicholas Hilliard wrote on the border of his portrait of Francis Bacon at 18. At that age, Francis had already attended Cambridge for three years, become disillusioned with its stifling atmosphere, entered Gray's Inn to study law, and spent three years in the court of France.

De Augmentis and *Novum Organum*. This is made even more astounding by the fact that Roger's *Opus* was never published in his lifetime, fell into oblivion, and not until 113 years after Francis' *Novum Organum* and 110 years after his *De Augmentis* did it appear in print!

The unsurpassed wit of this immortal soul, this philosopher/king, this priest/scientist, might easily have kept its humor with the stubborn motto drawn from tyrants, tortures and tragedy: If they beat you in one life, come back and beat them in the next!

Francis Bacon is known as the father of inductive reasoning and the scientific method, which, more than any other contributions, are responsible for the age of technology in which we now live. He foreknew that only applied science could free the masses from human misery and the drudgery of sheer survival in order that they might seek a higher spirituality they once knew. Thus, science and technology were essential to Saint Germain's plan for the liberation of his lightbearers and through them all mankind.

His next step was to be nothing less bold than universal enlightenment!

"The Great Instauration" (restoration after decay, lapse, or dilapidation) was his formula to change "the whole wide world." First conceived when Bacon was a boy of 12 or 13 and later crystallized in 1607 in his book by the same name, it did indeed launch the English Renaissance with the help of Francis' tender, caring person. For over the years, he gathered around himself a group of brilliant men who were responsible among other things for almost all of the Elizabethan literature—Ben Jonson, John Davies, George Herbert, John Selden, Edmund Spenser, Sir Walter Raleigh, Gabriel Harvey, Robert Greene, Sir Philip Sidney, Christopher Marlowe, John Lyly, George Peele, and Lancelot Andrewes.

Some of these were part of a "secret society" that Francis had formed with his brother, Anthony, when the two were law students at Gray's Inn. This fledgling group, called "The Knights of the Helmet," had as its goal the advancement of learning by expanding the English language and by creating a new literature written not in Latin but in words which Englishmen could understand.

Francis Bacon, 1st Viscount St Alban, by John Vanderbank

Francis Bacon sponsored the early society of the Rosy Cross, the Rosicrucian Order, and was instrumental in founding the Masonic Order. From his famous *New Atlantis,* the Masons derive their heritage of the House of Solomon and the Masonic tradition of America as the Promised Land where golden-age culture and science will rise again.

Francis also organized the translation of the King James Version of the Bible, determined that the common people should have the benefit of reading God's Word for themselves. Furthermore, as was discovered in the 1890s in two separate ciphers—a word-cipher and a bi-literal cipher embedded in the type of the original printings of the Shakespearean Folios[16]—Francis Bacon *was* the author of the plays attributed to the actor from the squalid village of Stratford-on-Avon. He was the greatest literary genius of the Western world.

So, too, was Bacon behind many of the political ideas on which Western civilization is based. Thomas Hobbes, John Locke and Jeremy Bentham took Bacon as their ideological starting point. His revolutionary principles are the engine that has driven the American nation. They are the very essence of the can-do spirit. "Men are not animals erect," Bacon averred, "but immortal Gods. The Creator has given us souls equal to all the world, and yet satiable not even with a world."[17]

Francis Bacon also continued the task he had begun as Christopher Columbus, promoting the colonization of the New World, for he knew that it was there that his ideas could take deepest root and come to fullest flower. He convinced James I to charter Newfoundland and was an officer in the Virginia Company, which sponsored the settlement of Jamestown, England's first permanent colony in America. And he founded Freemasonry, dedicated to the freedom and enlightenment of mankind, whose members played a large part in founding the new nation.

Yet he could have been an even greater boon to England and the whole world had he been allowed to fulfill his destiny. The same ciphers that run throughout the Shakespearean plays also run through Francis Bacon's own works and those of many of his circle of friends. Both ciphers contain his true life story, the musings of his soul, and anything he wished to bequeath to future generations but could not publish openly for fear of the queen.[18]

Its secrets reveal that he should have been Francis I, King of England. He was the son of Queen Elizabeth I and Robert Dudley, Lord Leicester, born four months after a secret wedding ceremony. But she, wishing to retain her "Virgin Queen" status and afraid that if she acknowledged her marriage, she must give power to the ambitious Leicester, also lest the people prefer her male heir to herself and demand the queen's premature withdrawal from the throne, refused to allow Francis, on pain of death, to assume his true identity.

The queen kept him dangling all his life, never giving him public office, never proclaiming him her son, never allowing him to fulfill his goals for England. No, she would not allow her son to bring in the golden age of Britannia that was meant to be but never was. What cruel fate—a queen mother unbending, contemptuous before her golden-age prince!

He was raised the foster son of Sir Nicholas and Lady Anne Bacon and at age fifteen heard the truth of his birth from his own mother's lips in the same breath with which she barred him forever from the succession. In one night, his world was in a shambles. Like young Hamlet, he pondered over and over the question, "To be or not to be?" That was *his* question.

In the end, he determined not to rebel against his mother or later, against her ill-fitted successor, James I. This despite the great good he knew he could bring to England, despite his vision of the land "as she might be, if wisely governed."[19] He knew he had within himself the power to be a monarch such as the land had never known, a true father of the nation. He wrote of the "impulses of the godlike patriarchal care for his own people" he would exercise[20]—shades of the golden-age emperor of the Sahara.

Fortunately for the world, Francis determined to pursue his goal of universal enlightenment in the avenues of literature and science, as adviser to the throne, supporter of colonization, and founder of secret societies, thereby reestablishing the thread of contact with the ancient mystery schools. The outlet of his wounded spirit was his cipher writing, into which he poured out his longings to a future age.

Thus from a celestial visitation he took his lead as he was led to achieve his immortality by truth's rhyme and not by kingly fame. Athena, the original "spear shaker,"[21] was his Muse and Patroness— thus the Shakespearean plays truly received their name.

FROM ADEPT TO ASCENDED MASTER

By the time of his death in 1626, persecuted and unrecognized for his manifold talents, Francis Bacon had triumphed over circumstances that would have destroyed lesser men, but which for him proved the true making of an ascended master.

> Enter Saint Germain May 1, 1684,
> God of Freedom to the earth.
> Draped with a cloak of stars,
> He stands with his twin flame,
> The Goddess of Justice,
> Against the backdrop of cosmos.
> He is come to ignite the fires of world
>   transmutation
> In hearts attuned to the cosmic cyphers
> And to avert personal and planetary cataclysm.
> He pleads the cause of God-freedom
> Before the councils of men
> And presents his case before
> The world body of lightbearers.
> He offers a ransom for the oppressed—
> Gift of his heart—and of his mind,
> Rarest jewel of all our earthly souvenirs—

And of his causal body:
Sphere upon sphere of the richness of himself
Harvested from the divine, and the human,
    experience.

All this he offers.
Like a beggar with his bowl piled high,
He plies the streets of the world
Eyeing passersby
Hopeful that even one in every million
Might take the proffered gift
And hold it to his heart in recognition
Of the Source, of the Sun,
And of the alchemy of the age so close.
Yes, as close as free will and the divine spark
Is our extrication from the dilemma
Of doubt and deleterious concepts and death.
And as far, as far as the toiler's envy
Of our love tryst is from grace,
So, without him, is the morning of our deliverance
From tangled entanglements of karmic crisscrosses
Of our doodling and dabbling for centuries'
    boredom
With personalities far less, oh yes, than his.

Enter Saint Germain
Into our hearts forever, if we will only let him.

THE WONDERMAN OF EUROPE

May 1, 1684, was Saint Germain's Ascension Day. From heights of power well-earned and beyond this world's, he still stands to turn back all attempts to thwart his "Great Instauration" here below.

Desiring above all else to liberate God's people, whether they would be liberated or not, Saint Germain sought and was granted a dispensation from the Lords of Karma to return to earth in a physical body. He appeared as "le Comte de Saint Germain," a "miraculous" gentleman who dazzled the courts of eighteenth- and nineteenth-century Europe, where they called him "The Wonderman." And with good reason. Never had anyone so captured the attention of an entire continent quite like this Monsieur. He was, as Voltaire described him, the "man who never dies and who knows everything."

But that was incomplete. He was also the man who could play the violin "like an orchestra." The man who spoke flawless French, English, Italian, Spanish, and Portuguese—who was an expert in

Latin, Greek, Chinese, Sanskrit, and Arabic. The man who was a poet, painter and artisan; scholar, statesman, and raconteur.

He was no mythical figure spun out of salon gossip. Frederick the Great, Voltaire, Horace Walpole and Casanova mentioned him in their letters. Newspapers of the day—*The London Chronicle* of June 1760, *Le notizie del Mondo,* a Florentine newspaper in July of 1770, and *The Gazette of the Netherlands*—took note of him.

Madame du Hausset, *femme de chambre* to Madame de Pompadour, wrote of him at some length in her memoirs. She tells how in 1757 he undertook to remove a flaw from a medium-sized diamond for Louis XV. After weighing the diamond, she wrote, "his Majesty said to the Comte: 'The value of this diamond as it is, and with the flaw in it, is six thousand livres; without the flaw it would be worth at least ten thousand. Will you undertake to make me a gainer of four thousand livres?'

"Saint Germain examined it very attentively, and said, 'It is possible; it may be done. I will bring it to you again in a month.'

The Count of St. Germain, engraving by Nicolas Thomas

"At the time appointed the Comte de St. Germain brought back the diamond without a spot, and gave it to the King. It was wrapped in a cloth of amianthos, which he took off. The king had it weighed immediately, and found it very little diminished. His Majesty then sent it to his jeweller . . . without telling him of anything that had passed. The jeweller gave him nine thousand six hundred livres for it. The King, however, sent for the diamond back again, and said he would keep it as a curiosity."

The King, of course, was astonished. He made the remark that "M. de St. Germain must be worth millions, especially if he possessed the secret of making large diamonds out of small ones."

The sources of the Wonderman's income and his net worth were never discovered. Clearly he was a man of extraordinary means. One countess wrote that even though he dressed plainly, he wore an abundance of diamonds—on every finger, on his watch, on his shoe buckles. The finest diamonds even adorned his snuff box. But as for making diamonds grow, Madame du Hausset tells us that "the Comte neither said that he could or could not, but positively asserted that he knew how to make pearls grow, and give them the finest water."

There seemed, in fact, no end to the things he could do. The Marquis de Valbelle reported seeing him change a silver six-franc piece into gold. In a letter dated 1763, Count Karl Cobenzl asserted that the Count Saint Germain had performed "under my own eyes . . . the transmutation of iron into a metal as beautiful as gold."

How did he do it? Many would have liked to have known the Count's secrets—kings, ministers, diplomats, mystics, and savants. Some, no doubt, desired to enrich themselves. Others sought his ruin —for the Wonderman had his enemies. But whatever their purpose, no one ever discovered anything about him he did not wish them to know. The Count was a man of mystery.

No one knew quite where he came from nor how old he was, although there was a great deal of speculation about the matter. For the 112 years, beginning in 1710, that European society reported seeing him, the Wonderman appeared to be about 45 years of age. But when asked, he would graciously decline to reveal his date of birth. To one countess he would admit only that he was very old.

Sometimes he appeared to be jesting. Or was he reading from *akasha?* Madame de Pompadour wrote that he would describe scenes from the court of Valois [fourteenth to sixteenth century] in such precise and minute detail as to give the unmistakable impression that he had been there.

The Wonderman was reputed to have concocted medicines which prolonged his life and to know the secret of the elixir of life. One memoir-writer said that he gave such an elixir to Madame v. Georgy "which for fully a quarter of a century preserved unaltered the youthful charms she possessed at 25."

Nor were these the end of the Count's wonders. His manners were exquisite and he was a brilliant, although sometimes enigmatic, conversationalist. Madame d'Adhémar, confidante of Marie Antoinette, reported seeing him vanish outside the royal quarters at Versailles. Cornelius van Sypesteyn wrote that he could "tame bees and make snakes listen to music." Such feats known to Indian yogis alike, nevertheless did not detract from his remarkableness.

But to what end were the Count's labors? A man with infinite wealth and eternal life has no need to impress. The truth of the matter is, he had a number of goals, including dispersing the gathering storm that eventually burst forth on Europe as the French Revolution.

The Count had the ability to describe the future with the same precision with which he recalled the past. He saw the French Revolution coming long before the Reign of Terror and the guillotine when blood flowed in the streets of Paris.

But he certainly did not think it was an unalterable event. No, indeed. "A gigantic conspiracy is being formed, which as yet has no visible chief, but he will appear before long," he told Madame d'Adhémar some years before the revolution, when the French throne was the most splendid institution in Europe. She recorded his prophecy in her diary: "The aim is nothing less than the overthrow of what exists, to reconstruct it on a new plan. There is ill-will towards the royal family, the clergy, the nobility, the magistracy. There is still time, however, to baffle the plot; later, this would be impossible."

Apparently, the Wonderman had it in mind to help effect a smooth transition from monarchical to republican forms of government. He knew the old order was passing and labored to establish a United States of Europe before the French Revolution would ultimately leave nothing good nor bad of her royal houses.

The Count Saint Germain tried to warn Louis XVI of the webs of intrigue being woven around the monarchy, Madame d'Adhémar reported. First he explained to Marie Antoinette what would take place. He then begged her to tell the king and arrange a meeting between the two of them without the presence of the king's chief adviser, Monsieur de Maurepas.

Madame d'Adhémar, present at the meeting between the Wonderman and Marie Antoinette, recorded his words: "Some years yet will pass by in a deceitful calm; then from all parts of the kingdom will spring up men greedy for vengeance, for power, and for money; they will overthrow all in their way.... Civil war will burst out with all its horrors; it will bring in its train murder, pillage, exile. Then it will be regretted that I was not listened to."

Alas, it is not only in his own country that a prophet may be without honor. Maurepas, a bitter enemy of the Count Saint Germain, intervened. King and Count never met. The rest is history.

There is much more to tell, of course. But many of the things that could be said are already included in the opening section of *Saint Germain On Alchemy,* entitled "The Wonderman of Europe." They also appear in *The Comte de Saint Germain,* by Isabel Cooper-Oakley. The latter, for the most part, is a collection of eyewitness accounts of the Count Saint Germain's amazing works drawn from letters and diaries, family archives, and state papers, including the secret diplomatic correspondence files of the British National Record Office.

"Thus clearly stands out the character of one who by some is called a 'messenger' from that spiritual hierarchy by whom the world's evolution is guided," Cooper-Oakley concluded. "Such is the moral worth of the man whom the shallow critics of the earth called 'adventurer.'"

The charge of charlatanry was no doubt born as often of jealousy of his powers as disbelief in his miracles. The Count Saint Germain was accused in his own time, without foundation, by an unnamed group of Jesuits of "immorality, infidelity, anarchy" and, because of his work with alchemists and the Masons, by Abbé Barruel and later Nesta Webster, of being a magician in league with various nefarious secret societies seeking the overthrow of France, including the Bavarian Illuminati founded in 1776 by Adam Weishaupt.

Since 1786, when the Illuminati were exposed and suppressed by the Bavarian government, it has been well known that it was a subversive organization which was deceptively grafted onto the body of Masonry by Weishaupt and Baron von Knigge, that it was anti-religious and anti-monarchical in outlook, that it desperately opposed the goals and philosophy of Masonry. Furthermore, it was thought by some to have played a crucial role in fomenting the French Revolution. Barruel's and Webster's accusations apparently rise from their general misunderstanding of the history of secret societies and the Count Saint Germain's mystical powers.

Some criticism of the Count was spawned from nothing more than seeds of superstition born of fear. Case in point: Saint Germain has told us of how he walked through the streets of Paris healing children from a disease similar to poliomyelitis. At his touch, they would recover almost instantly— and yet their mothers would jerk them from his grasp and call him *diable*—devil.

But, as we have seen, the most painful denouement for the Wonderman was that he could not secure the necessary response from those who could have turned the tide in the affairs of men and nations. The royalty were willing to be entertained by the adept but not to relinquish their power and move with the winds of democratic change. They and their jealous ministers ignored his counsel and opened the door to the war and bloodshed that has resounded through the centuries since.

In a final attempt to unite Europe, Saint Germain backed Napoleon, who misused the Master's power to his own demise. The opportunity to set aside the retribution due an age thus passed, Saint Germain was once again forced to withdraw from a karmic situation. In this episode, though clearly visible as the mediator, Saint Germain with his miracles in hand and his prophecies fulfilled could still be ignored!

Well, as suddenly as the Count Saint Germain burst onto the stage of Europe he disappeared. Or perhaps it is more accurate to say that after 1822— the date of his last recorded appearance—he simply stopped appearing.

In the latter eighteenth century, he told Franz Gräffer and Baron Linden he would go to "rest" in the Himalayas. In 1875, Saint Germain helped the masters M. (El Morya), K.H. (Koot Hoomi), and Serapis Bey found the Theosophical Society. But that was not all.

THE FOUNDING OF AMERICA

Throughout the period of his labors as "the Comte," Saint Germain had been constantly in service in various "far-off lands," including one that became a hotbed of revolution—a rustic land that would eventually be called the United States of America. He has told us:

> Having failed in securing the attention of the Court of France and others of the crowned heads of Europe, I turned myself to the perfectionment of mankind at large, and I recognized that there were many who, hungering and thirsting after righteousness, would indeed be filled with the concept of a perfect union which would inspire them to take dominion over the New World and create a

Union among the sovereign states. Thus the United States was born as a child of my heart and the American Revolution was the means of bringing freedom in all of its glory into manifestation from the East unto the West.[22]

Even as Francis Bacon, he had seen America as his last hope. He wrote in cipher, "I trusteth all to the future and a land that is very far towards the sunset gate.... I keep the future ever in my plan, looking for my reward, not to my times or countrymen, but to a people very far off, and an age not like our own, but a second golden age of learning."[23]

In "The Mystical Origins of the United States of America," an article that appears in *Saint Germain On Alchemy*, the role Saint Germain played behind the scenes in founding the United States of America is described in detail. He inspired the Masons with the vision of a union of sovereign states in a new order of the ages. He stood by George Washington throughout the Revolution and during the long winter at Valley Forge. He inspired and directed the writing of the Constitution and anointed Washington first president of the United States.

UNVEILING THE SECRET FIRE

Now, once again, the earth is at a crossroads. Once again, the hierarch of the Aquarian age is trying to assist mankind to avoid catastrophes that could dwarf those that occurred when his warnings as the Count Saint Germain were not heeded.

As Saint Germain explained:

> I have also walked the earth in time of chaos as the Wonderman of Europe. I have demonstrated a path and a mastery, yet none could relate to it. For the books were not written, the violet-flame dispensation had not come nor the opportunity to give to the masses of the people by mass communication the understanding of the science of decrees. There was no means whereby the rank and file or the royalty themselves could follow a path in my footsteps. All they could have was the stamping upon their memory of my demonstration of alchemical feats.[24]

In the last century Saint Germain went before the Lords of Karma with the proposal to make the knowledge of the violet flame available to all mankind. As collateral for this dispensation, Saint Germain offered his own personal momentum of the seventh ray that he had garnered for thousands of years. The scientific use of the violet flame in this age has been made possible by Saint Germain so that we could experiment with the alchemy of self-transformation through the sacred fire.

The knowledge of the violet flame had never been given outside the retreats of the ascended masters. The Lords of Karma agreed, however, to release it to a certain nucleus of devotees. If the experiment proved successful, they would illumine the masses as to its uses. In the early 1930s, therefore, Saint Germain founded the I AM Activity and released the dispensation of the violet flame.

When mankind en masse failed to respond, the Lords of Karma told Saint Germain they would not give him "another allotment of energy for mankind to take and to dissipate and to waste." In Saint Germain's own words, "after seventy thousand years of sponsoring various endeavors for the enlightenment and the freedom of mankind...my wings were clipped. And I had but to stand and hope that some other hierarch would come forth to implore a dispensation of light for humanity, for souls of light."[25]

In 1958, El Morya, on Saint Germain's behalf, founded The Summit Lighthouse for the release and publication of the teachings of the ascended masters and the establishment of the community of the Holy Spirit in the Aquarian age. Saint Germain anointed Mark and Elizabeth Prophet as his messengers and sponsored the Keepers of the Flame Fraternity.

On September 3, 1973, Saint Germain announced: "As a result of the swelling of the lightbearers and the swelling of the ranks of students of light united in this activity, . . . I have been given again a dispensation from the Lords of Karma! Thus I may once again step forth and pledge to you the energies of my causal body for the freedom and the victory of the light in this age!"

2

A SACRED FIRE:
THE VIOLET TRANSMUTING
FLAME

The violet flame is the energy of freedom. People who are free have the violet light vibrating in their auras—unmistakably. The violet flame is also an energy of mercy and forgiveness. And transmutation.

Transmutation means to change—to alter in form, appearance, or nature. The term was used by medieval alchemists who attempted to transmute base metals into gold, separating the "subtle" from the "gross" by means of heat.

That is precisely what the energy of the Holy Spirit does. It is a tangible emanation of spiritual fire that actually "melts" the "elements" of our subconscious "with fervent heat"—as the Bible says.

This is the way to undo psychological problems, emotional hang-ups, records of the past. We don't have to go back through hypnosis or regression. Send the love-fire of the Holy Spirit through—and it all begins to change by the alchemy of the violet transmuting flame.

Saint Germain says:

> Seldom do mankind realize the glorious wisdom of the mind of God that has contrived the violet transmuting flame in all of its cosmic unfolding glory. It is difficult for the world in its present state of development to fully comprehend from the level of the human consciousness or through the power of the human mind those momentous, invisible actions and activities of the sacred fires of God.
>
> When the average individual calls the violet transmuting flame into action, he does not have the power to perceive the dancing stream of electrons which perform on the state of his consciousness, nor is he aware of the tremendous cosmic energy

involved therein. You do not realize this great potential that transcends both time and space and produces in the now of your life's adventure a blessed action of transmutation or cosmic change that moves you a step forward on the path.[1]

The violet flame has always been used in the inner retreats of the Brotherhood. Up until now, it has been reserved for the privileged few—those initiates who were found worthy—members of secret societies, or communicants of the flame in the mystery schools.

THE PHILOSOPHER'S STONE

Early alchemists pored over minutely ciphered texts in search of the mystic-magical philosopher's stone. For them it was worth a lifetime to decode the mystery of this stone, which symbolized "the transmutation of the lower animal nature into the highest and divine."

Theosophical alchemists gloried in the vision of a "secret flame." The coveted philosopher's stone, "the Stone which is no stone," was not physical but spiritual and created out of fire!

According to Neoplatonist predecessors of medieval alchemy, it was a sacrificial, self-transforming fire that would lead the soul upward—and, in the process, transmute the "hard and refractory materials" in the human body to materials more luminous and rarefied. In this sacred experiment, the alchemist would become "like the gods," pursuing what one seventeenth-century text called "the gold of the wise and not the vulgar metal."

Sacrificial fire, the texts explain, leads up to the "fire of the gods" by drawing upward to the Spirit all qualities that drag downward and oppose the celestial essences. Transmutation, then, was a spiritual process that exalted the soul into a state of unity with the Divine.

Now (thanks to Saint Germain) you can begin to experience the action of this sacrificial fire—the violet fire—passing over the pages of the subconscious record of your incarnations on earth. The violet fire is sacred "secret" fire. It penetrates the most secret little places of our mind and memory. It comes in, sweeps through—and, with a roaring crackle, sweeps out the dust of centuries. Line by line, letter by letter, the flame—intelligent, luminous, directed by the mind of God—sets free the energies, electron by electron, of our past misuse of the sacred fire, thereby restoring the natural resource of the inner light.

ANCIENT KNOWLEDGE

Isaac Newton observed that a ray of sunlight, when passed through a prism, will separate into the seven colors of the rainbow: red, orange, yellow, green, blue, indigo, violet. This visible light is only a tiny portion of an electromagnetic spectrum of varying frequencies or wavelengths that include radio waves, infrared radiation, ultraviolet rays, X-rays, gamma rays. Today, scientists know of 60 to 70 octaves of light.

Violet, with the shortest wavelength, has the highest frequency in the visible spectrum and is at the point of transition to the next octave of light. To the ancients, this transitional, transcendental color was a spiritual rather than a physical phenomenon.

Egypt cherished the deep violet amethyst as a soothing, a healing stone, even as divine protection from evil. The Greek historian Lucian describes a fabled city of gems—whose altars are enormous blocks of amethyst.

Homer's *Odyssey* was sung by bards ceremoniously wrapped in precious purples. Agamemnon's wife rolled out a purple-crimson carpet to greet him home from Troy—"tinted splendors," noted the king, reserved only for the gods. Caesar also craved the costly color as the mantle of the supreme god, Jupiter.

When Pilate's soldiers plaited the crown of thorns for Jesus "King of the Jews," they also put on him a purple robe. Thus purple became symbolic of mystic "suffering," sacrifice, and penance. And violet was designated for liturgical vestments during the seasons of purgation—Advent and Lent.

Behind the scenes of visible color and light, mystics of all ages, East and West, have glimpsed a "spiritual spectrum." Radiant colors, purer and more rare than those of earth, emanate from a brilliant white "inner" light that is divine in nature.

Scholars are beginning to see ancient "sun worshipers" as devotees of this transphysical spiritual light—the divine sun that illumines the inner world, "the Sun behind the sun."

The Zohar, an important work of the Jewish Kabbalah, affirms that "there exists a sort of fire which is stronger than other fire.... Above the white light and encompassing it is yet another light, this one symbolizing the supreme essence."

Zarathustra witnessed the creation of all things from a single fire. Mithraic prayers adore the Lord of Light as the "Fire-hearted One... whose Body is of Fire."

"In a flame of fire" the angel of the Lord appeared unto Moses. And out of that flaming flame was the contact of a soul with his own higher consciousness. Based on that experience, Moses told the children of Israel: "The LORD thy God is a consuming fire!"

And Jesus Christ summed up his mission in nine words: "I am come to send fire on the earth."

While in a state of ecstasy in dialogue with God the Father, Saint Catherine of Siena dictated these words: "I, Fire, Acceptor of sacrifices, ravishing away from them their darkness, give the light; not a natural light, but a supernatural...."

John of the Cross was inwardly transformed in the "living flame" of love. "Such is the activity of the Holy Spirit in the soul," he writes. "The interior acts He produces shoot up flames for they are acts of inflamed love."

THE SEVEN RAYS

Esoteric researcher H. P. Blavatsky describes the divine light in terms of seven colors, or "rays"— each of which has specific attributes or qualities. The violet flame comes forth from that aspect of the white light that is called the "seventh ray."

Just as sunlight passing through a prism is refracted into the rainbow of the seven rays, so in the consciousness of the Holy Spirit the light of the Christ is refracted for our use in the matter plane.

Each of the seven rays is a concentrated action of the light of God having a specific color and frequency resulting in a specific action in body, mind, and soul. The violet flame is the specific of the Holy Spirit, the antidote, that dissolves the delusions of the pseudo-self—and even the laws of old age and death. It is the fulfillment of the prophecy of God's own law of transmutation "Though your sins be as scarlet, they shall be as white as snow; though they be red like crimson, they shall be as wool."

The violet flame does not destroy, for the Law

is precise: God's energy is neither created nor destroyed. The violet flame *changes* the water into wine. It strips atoms and molecules of the dense overlay of human imperfection and restores the natural divine perfection of the soul and its original desire to be whole.

3

THE UNIVERSAL SOLVENT
OF THE VIOLET FLAME

Now let us examine what happens when the specific of the violet fire is applied to the accumulation of karma in the subconscious:

Instantaneously, the fire begins the work of breaking down particles of substance that are part of hundreds and even thousands of incarnations. Believe it or not, this energy can be as hard as concrete as it fills the wide-open spaces between the electrons and the nuclei of the atoms, causing mental recalcitrance, hardness of heart, a lack of sensitivity to the needs of others—and creating a dense mass that prevents the soul from receiving the delicate impartations of the Holy Spirit.

Man is a microcosm—a miniature representation of the cosmos. Just as there is a vast space between the planets and the sun, so there is vast space between the electrons and the nucleus inside every cell and atom of your body consciousness.

The space between the electron and the fiery nucleus is known as "virgin" or "hallowed" space. It is filled with the pulsating energy of the Holy Spirit. It is essence—an essence of God.

We are constantly using this vital essence that is between the electrons and the nucleus of the atom. We are constantly qualifying that energy— stamping it with the impressions of our minds and hearts. And this is how densification occurs.

You can imagine filling the space between electrons with molasses—a sticky astral glue that blocks the flow of light from the Macrocosm of God to the microcosm of man. What happens to the electrons? They slow down. They can't pass through.

That is, in effect, what we've been doing for hundreds of thousands of years. We have been filling the space between the electrons with discord, with a lack of wholeness—call it what you will. Call it "bad karma." Call it "sin" if you must. Essentially any manifestation of imperfection fills that "hallowed" space with density.

PHYSICAL ALCHEMY

Dr. Bernard Jensen reported that hatred and other negative thoughts and feelings actually create acids (excess amounts of phosphoric acid, uric acid, and carbonic acid gases) that the body cannot assimilate. Hence the density of disease persists within the physical orbit.

Atoms of consciousness have become so polluted that our environment is now polluted as well. We have polluted the atoms of air, polluted the atoms of earth, polluted the atoms of water—not simply with chemicals but with our thoughts and feelings. Physical pollution is but an effect of mental and emotional pollution. Therefore, to solve the problem of pollution, we must restore the native flow of the Holy Spirit.

That's the science of it. The dilemma is, How do we speed up our electrons? By removing the effluvia that is caught between those wide-open spaces. How? There is only one way. By using the same energies that we have misused—the energies of the Holy Spirit.

The accelerating, violet-flame energy of the

Holy Spirit envelops each atom individually. Can you imagine what a tiny particle of substance an atom is? Yet the flame of God caresses and wraps each atom individually. Instantaneously, a polarity is set up between the white-fire core of the atom (which, being matter, assumes the negative pole) and the white-fire core of the flame (which, being spirit, assumes the positive pole).

The dual action of the sacred fire within the center of the atom and the violet flame without establishes a forcefield that causes the untransmuted densities to be dislodged from between the electrons. As this substance is loosed, the electrons begin to spin more rapidly in their orbits—and by centrifugal force it is thrown into the violet flame. On contact with this fiery essence of freedom's flame, the misqualified energy is transmuted into its native purity.

THE WINE OF FORGIVENESS

The violet flame is the spiritual wine of forgiveness, the quality of mercy that, as Shakespeare wrote, "is not strain'd," that "droppeth as the gentle rain from heaven upon the place beneath:

it is twice blest; it blesseth him that gives and him that takes."

That "giving" and "taking" is the constant of flow. Flow is the interaction of energy between God and man. Flow is the return to the Source of energy so that that Source can release more energy.

All of cosmos depends for its very existence upon that flow. When you stop the flow, you have death, disease, disintegration. *Disintegration*—the "dis-integration" of the atom that is devoid of the integrating essence of the Holy Spirit.

If we can't let go to this cosmic flow, this mighty movement of the Spirit of God, then we have lost the essential reason for being—for life itself. That is why the violet flame brings such feelings of joy, lightness, hope, and newness of life. It restores the flow. And with the restoration of the macrocosmic/ microcosmic flow, it is as though clouds of depression were being dissolved by the very sun of our own being.

When the spirit of man flows into the Spirit of God and the Spirit of God flows into the spirit of man, there is a divine exchange—a cosmic transmutation—and both God and man enjoy the feeling of sharing and of belonging to one another.

"All problems of the economy, the ecology, and the government can be resolved," Saint Germain says, "if you will take only ten minutes each day to go within and to find your own God Self, to meditate and to use the science of the spoken Word whereby you chant the mantra of the free:

> *I AM a being of violet fire—*
> *I AM the purity God desires!*

"This is my mantra which I give to you as your initiation into the Aquarian age."

> *I AM a being of violet fire—*
> *I AM the purity God desires!*

The sacred name *I AM* releases the fire locked in the nucleus of the permanent atom of Self.

4

THE NAME OF GOD

Remember when Moses was on the mountain and there was a bush that burned but was not consumed—and then God called to him out of the midst of the burning bush? Moses understood God as fire. But at the precise moment that God reveals himself as an energy, as that flaming flame—at that moment the LORD God steps right through that energy and becomes a person talking with Moses face-to-face. The energy speaks. It becomes an identity, an individuality—the very person of the Holy Spirit.

When you look at the nature of energy, you realize that it is always simultaneously principle and person. Principle and person is simply the plus and minus polarity. The positive polarity becomes negative as the negative polarity realizes individuality.

God is the cloven tongues of fire—Spirit-Matter. Spirit represents the principle of universal energy. Matter represents that energy becoming a person. By the law of polarity, that which is principle *must* become person. It is a lesson in science and mathematics.

Moses had that experience. Energy became person—a person that was a friend. God manifested himself as friend and talked with Moses face-to-face out of that burning bush. Why? To initiate his mission in life.

What does initiation mean? It means that God imparts to us as individuals an increment of light, or energy, which enters into our soul and gives us a push, a thrust, a consciousness, an idea, an awareness. It's like wind in our sails.

So Moses stood there and the voice spoke out of the flame and the LORD God said to him: "Let my people go!" God is sending Moses to rescue the people of Israel from a false sense of freedom, a very entrenched materialism. But Moses was very timid. He feared. He doubted his own ability.

Moses trembles before that person—as we would also tremble before the sacred fire. He said,

"I'm not qualified. The people will not listen to me. Perhaps if they know who sent me they will listen to me—someone, perhaps, more powerful than I. Whom shall I say sent me? By whose authority shall I deliver this word? Who are you, anyway?"

The resounding Word that comes back is the resounding Word that we hear in our own inner being— the declaration of the Presence of God where we are. The voice of the LORD speaks out of that flame to Moses and says: I AM THAT I AM. I AM WHO I AM. I will be what I will be. OM TAT SAT OM.

The name of God I AM THAT I AM is a key to energy. Every time you use "I AM" you are declaring, "God in me is." It is an affirmation of your true Self. It releases the fire of your heart to fulfill the destiny to which you send it forth. This is more than the power of positive thinking. Make no mistake. This is the alchemy of the sacred fire.

"I AM" is a loaded word. It is loaded with the power of the nucleus of your being. If you say, "I am well, I am happy, I am whole," the fire leaps and makes a cycle through your mind and heart and soul (and when you say the reverse, you create the consequences).

> *I AM a being of violet fire—*
> *I AM the purity God desires!*

When you give this mantra, the flow of the Word goes forth in a clockwise spiral around your being. And you, as a pillar of energy, become a coil of the fire of freedom.

In the flow of the mantra, the stepping-up of the tempo corresponds to the stepping-up of the vibration of the light flowing through you. When you let God speak the Word through you, the natural flow of light intensifies the flow of the mantra.

> *I AM a being of violet fire—*
> *I AM the purity God desires!*

This is an example of how the white-fire core receives all back unto itself. All of the colors—the rainbow rays of the prism of God's consciousness—return to the white-fire core. And the violet flame becomes the white light as the mantra converges in the AUM.

> *I AM a being of violet fire—*
> *I AM the purity God desires!*
> *AUM*

THE TONE OF OUR IDENTITY

Scientists now recognize the fact that each individual has his own "cosmic clock." We each have a unique vibration. That vibration consists of the frequencies of all of our atoms and molecules.

All our atoms and molecules put together make the "tone" of identity, which we recognize when we greet our friends, when we have affinities (and perhaps repulsions) for one another. Those "vibes" —that frequency—have to do with how the Word is flowing.

When the flame of freedom comes into being and you become that flame, you have a new pitch, a new sound, a new consciousness. And as you increase the tempo of the mantra, you are controlling a whole cosmos of atoms and molecules and energy fields.

We begin slowly, controlling each word as we control each electron. Then we step it up and we find that we can maintain control at an increased vibration—just as man has conquered movement in time and space, securing inventions for greater and greater speed and finally breaking the barrier of sound. This we do by the control of the Word and the science of the Word.

Experiment with the mantra. If you do not exercise the power of the spoken Word, you will be an island in the midst of a sea of flame. For by free will that flame cannot coalesce and form that spiral if you do not give the fiat. This is the law of free will and of the science of the spoken Word. The flame is unknown until you make it your own.

MAKE THE VIOLET FLAME YOUR OWN

This is a simple mantra that you can accelerate and accelerate and give it as a perpetual prayer on your lips as you go about your daily life.

> *I AM a being of violet fire—*
> *I AM the purity God desires!*

Start getting rid of the consciousness of self as old, dense, feeble, ugly, stupid, bored, poor. All of a sudden you are "a being of violet fire." You're just a flaming flame—pulsating, moving with the Spirit. You move in a beautiful sea of violet flame.

As you give that mantra and accelerate and accelerate its speed—so you have the dissolving of the substance between the electrons and the nuclei. The electrons whirl faster and faster and faster. And you get lighter and lighter. Higher and higher.

This is a mantra you can use anytime, anywhere. You can make use of the Word within you instead of staying there in that same dense vibration—a victim of your circumstances in time and space. When you start feeling tense or irritated or tired or heavy or burdened during the day, just say a few "violet flames" and you'll be back into that cosmic flow.

Give it making breakfast, driving the car, washing the clothes—even taking a shower. Visualize your morning shower as a shower of violet flame. See the flame scrubbing the pores, passing through the nervous system, the arteries, the bloodstream—right down to the marrow of your bones.

And whatever you affirm for yourself, you can affirm for your city or for the entire nation. You can say your country or, *America is a land of violet fire—America is the purity God desires!* Simply change your visualization—like adjusting the lens of a camera. You can just as easily invoke enough violet flame to transmute the density of a city or a nation—or a planet or a solar system: *Earth is a planet of violet fire—Earth is the purity God desires!*

There is unbounded creativity in the violet flame! It liberates the energy of Aquarius in you— the full creativity of the Holy Spirit. It liberates love as the discipline of creative fires. Whatever your field, whatever your calling, you can take the sound, the rhythm, the energy, the Word—and feel yourself freer and freer.

The violet flame will unlock in you everything else that you have ever sought as consciousness and teaching and self-mastery. It's the key. It locks in everything else—because it transmutes the dross that impedes the flow of this stupendous light of the Holy Spirit.

5

THE POWER OF SOUND:
KEY TO THE MYSTERIES

R ecent scientific advances and studies point to what sages knew thousands of years ago: sound holds the key to the mysteries of the universe.

We know that sound can destroy—a high pitched note can shatter a wineglass, a sonic boom can crack plaster, a gunshot can set off an avalanche. But sound is also a constructive force, as doctors and health practitioners are discovering every day. Ultrasound (high-pitched sound waves) is being used for everything from cleaning wounds to diagnosing tumors to pulverizing kidney stones. Someday it may even be used to inject drugs into the body, making needles obsolete.

Scientists are now researching sound's impact on the brain. Certain kinds of classical music, by composers like Bach, Mozart and Beethoven, have a range of positive effects, including temporarily raising the IQ, expanding memory and speeding up learning. Some alternative health practitioners are experimenting with using specific tones to heal the organs.

The creative power of sound is also at the heart of the world's spiritual traditions East and West. Hindu writings tell us that yogis have used mantras, along with visualizations, to light fires, materialize physical objects (such as food), bring rain, and even influence the outcome of battles. Producing physical changes wasn't their primary goal, however. They believed that mantras brought them protection and wisdom, enhanced their concentration and meditation, and helped them achieve enlightenment and oneness with God.

The Jewish mystical tradition also speaks of the power of the spoken Word. Kabbalists believe that by calling upon and meditating on the names of God, we tap into an infinite source of power that restores peace and harmony to this world. They say that Moses, for instance, had the ability to "shake the world" because he called on the name of the LORD.

THE CHART OF YOUR DIVINE SELF

The reason we can call to God and he will answer is because we are connected to him. We are his sons and daughters. We have a direct relationship to God and he has placed a portion of himself in us. In order to better understand this relationship, the ascended masters have designed the Chart of Your Divine Self.

The Chart of Your Divine Self is a portrait of you and of the God within you. It is a diagram of yourself and your potential to become who you really are. It is an outline of your spiritual anatomy. The upper figure is your "I AM Presence," the Presence of God that is individualized in each one of us. It is your personalized "I AM THAT I AM."

Your I AM Presence is surrounded by seven concentric spheres of spiritual energy that make up what is called your "causal body." The spheres of pulsating energy contain the record of the good works you have performed since your very first incarnation on earth. They are like your cosmic bank account.

The Chart of Your Divine Self

THE HIGHER SELF

The middle figure in the Chart represents the "Holy Christ Self," who is also called the Higher Self. You can think of your Holy Christ Self as your chief guardian angel and dearest friend, your inner teacher and voice of conscience.

Just as the I AM Presence is the Presence of God that is individualized for each of us, so the Holy Christ Self is the presence of the universal Christ that is individualized for each of us. "The Christ" is actually a title given to those who have attained oneness with their Higher Self, or Christ Self. That's why Jesus was called "Jesus, the Christ." *Christ* comes from the Greek word *christos,* meaning "anointed"—anointed with the light of God.

What the Chart shows is that each of us has a Higher Self, or "inner Christ," and that each of us is destined to become one with that Higher Self—whether we call it the Christ, the Buddha, the Tao or the Atman. This "inner Christ" is what the Christian mystics sometimes refer to as the "inner man of the heart," and what the Upanishads mysteriously describe as a being the "size of a thumb" who "dwells deep within the heart."

We all have moments when we feel that connection with our Higher Self—when we are creative, loving, joyful. But there are other moments when we feel out of sync with our Higher Self—moments when we become angry, depressed, lost. What the spiritual path is all about is learning to sustain the connection to the higher part of ourselves so that we can make our greatest contribution to humanity.

THE DIVINE SPARK

The shaft of white light descending from the I AM Presence through the Holy Christ Self to the lower figure in the Chart is the crystal cord (sometimes called the silver cord). It is the "umbilical cord," the lifeline, that ties you to Spirit.

Your crystal cord also nourishes that special, radiant flame of God that is ensconced in the secret chamber of your heart. It is called the threefold flame, or divine spark, because it is literally a spark of sacred fire that God has transmitted from his heart to yours. This flame is called "threefold" because it engenders the primary attributes of Spirit —power, wisdom and love.

The mystics of the world's religions have

contacted the divine spark, describing it as the seed of divinity within. Buddhists, for instance, speak of the "germ of Buddhahood" that exists in every living being. In the Hindu tradition, the Katha Upanishad speaks of the "light of the Spirit" that is concealed in the "secret high place of the heart" of all beings.

Likewise, the fourteenth-century Christian theologian and mystic Meister Eckhart teaches of the divine spark when he says, "God's seed is within us." There is a part of us, says Eckhart, that "remains eternally in the Spirit and is divine. . . . Here God glows and flames without ceasing."

When we decree, we meditate on the flame in the secret chamber of our heart. This secret chamber is your own private meditation room, your interior castle, as Teresa of Avila called it. In Hindu tradition, the devotee visualizes a jeweled island in his heart. There he sees himself before a beautiful altar, where he worships his teacher in deep meditation.

Jesus spoke of entering the secret chamber of the heart when he said: "When thou prayest, enter into thy closet, and when thou hast shut thy door, pray to thy Father which is in secret; and thy Father which seeth in secret shall reward thee openly."

When I was a little girl I kept wondering: "What kind of closets did the disciples go into? Did people have closets in those days? You can't go into a closet —there's not enough air in there! What in the world is Jesus talking about?" Later on I realized that going into your closet to pray is going into another dimension of consciousness. It's entering into the heart and closing the door on the outside world.

YOUR SOUL'S POTENTIAL

The lower figure in the Chart of Your Divine Self represents you on the spiritual path, surrounded by the violet flame and the protective white light of God. The soul is the living potential of God—the part of you that is mortal but that can become immortal.

The purpose of your soul's evolution on earth is to grow in self-mastery, balance your karma[1] and fulfill your mission on earth so that you can return to the spiritual dimensions that are your real home. When your soul at last takes flight and ascends back to God and the heaven-world, you will become an "ascended" master, free from the rounds of karma and rebirth.

The high-frequency energy of the violet flame can help you reach that goal more quickly.

6

AN EXPERIENCE IN AN ETHERIC RETREAT

by the Darjeeling Master

The etheric retreats of the ascended masters serve many purposes. They are the homes of the masters in the heaven-world—the etheric body of planet Earth. The masters use the retreats to anchor certain energies throughout the earth on behalf of mankind. Records of past civilizations and golden ages are stored there. And perhaps most importantly, the masters serve in their retreats as the teachers of mankind. El Morya recounts in The Chela and the Path *the following experience of souls using the violet flame to heal past life trauma in his etheric retreat over Darjeeling, India.*

It is time to enter the chamber designed with blue and gold motif where there is a screen and seats arranged in theater style. For to understand your path, your very personal path to salvation, you must have the perspective of your past and how you have created the present—both at personal and planetary levels. Come then; and let us see how we shall, in the magic of the flame, discover the designs of your soul destiny.

We enter the chamber now and take our places before a large semicircular screen on which there will be projected the experiences of other incarnations. The group assembled here consists of unascended chelas—some of whom have an outer connection to Summit University. Others among the group are serving the will of God in their respective nations.

These look forward to the day when the teachings of the ascended masters will be published in their language, that they might read and study in their outer, waking consciousness that which they receive here in their finer bodies during sleep. One young couple taking their seats is accompanied by an unascended being of considerable attainment, of full stature and indeed recognized by the council. They will give birth to this soul in the not-too-distant future.

Scenes of life in ancient Thrace appear on the screen, and we find ourselves in the marketplace of a forgotten city in the land that is now Turkey. Two unascended masters walk midst the crowds unnoticed. The people are concerned with the activities of the day, with the purchase of food and supplies at the best prices, while the vendors carefully watch the passing of coins from hand to hand to see how much the day's business will bring. A group of devotees, including some now assembled in our retreat, enters the marketplace.

At the moment of their appearing, a peculiar astrological configuration aligns certain forces of hatred within the subconscious of the populace with an amalgamation of mass hatred focalized on astral planes. This interaction of forcefields we portray for those present, showing also the alignment of "fixed" and "wandering" stars. These energy fields amplify both the light and the darkness and cause the energizing of certain levels of karma in incarnations even prior to the ones now in focus on the screen.

Suddenly without warning, as if seized by a madness and a frenzy not entirely their own, certain individuals who seem to be at a random relationship to one another converge as a single entity. They act as a single unit—the mob—and with a single mind —the mass mind. They begin to pick up stones and hurl them at the devotees. The devotees are surrounded. Not terrified, but calmly centered in the flame that is the object of their worship, they shield their heads and their bodies. But to no avail.

The chelas' souls take leave of their finite forms, and the two unascended masters standing by raise the fohatic energies of their heart chakras to assist the souls in the transition. By karmic law they were not allowed to interfere with the circumstances that represented a converging of many forces and nature's demand for balance. Through their love and their mastery, they create a forcefield of light whereby the souls are taken safely to the etheric retreat of Pallas Athena over the island of Crete.

Now we roll back the drama on the screen so that all may examine the interplay of forces and the lines of karma that converged in the marketplace. They see how they themselves in a much earlier period of earth's history were drawn into acts of fanaticism that resulted in the death of those who retaliated that day in the forgotten city of ancient Thrace.

We review the scene in slow motion. I use the diamond that I wear on the index finger of my right hand to focus the action of the sacred fire on the screen. The violet ray that descends from the heart of my Presence is projected through the diamond and bursts forth as a thousand million flames on that scene on the screen. The chelas are on the edge of their seats as they watch the violet flame consume the cause and core, the record and memory—both in akasha and in their own subconscious.

The action of the violet flame intensifies in answer to my invocation made to the I AM Presence of each one: In the name of the Christ Self of the chelas, I invoke the fire of Almighty God to blaze forth the action of transmutation to change darkness into light—fear and hatred into love, envy into understanding, and vengeance into victory. As violet-flame angels from Zadkiel's retreat direct the energies of the flame, it forms coils of fire in the subconscious of each individual who was a party to this unfortunate interplay of energy.

Coils of fire are formed like the curly shavings that fall from planed wood. These coils rise and fall, rise and fall, intensifying the action of transmutation. And now they burst into a wide circle of energy and then return to the center. All of this is the action-formation of the fires of transmutation, flaming fire moving up and down and in and out; and then, following the circle of the cycles of individual karma in the electronic belt—a scrubbing action, a boiling action, a bubbling and a buoyant energy. Such is the diversity of the violet flame.

Scene by scene, step by step, the angels of the violet flame remove the record from the etheric body, the concepts from the mental body, the emotions from the feeling body, and the scars upon the physical matrix. Right before their very eyes, chelas of the will of God see what the glorious flame of God can do. They cheer. They applaud. And their bravos express the release of energy in their own hearts and a new freedom of the soul as this ancient record is cleared from their consciousness.

And now, in answer to the chelas' invocations to the violet flame, the fiery salamanders and the violet-flame angels, working hand in hand, retrace the record of that cycle when the lines of causation were drawn in the previous existence, which is also shown as chelas learn the lesson of blindly following the blind and of failing to invoke the wisdom of the Logos as a balance for the tyranny of the ego.

Mankind living in the world today assume that recorded history is what it is and that it cannot be changed.

They have not reckoned with the violet transmuting flame.

Those who attended the viewing in our retreat of the events at Thrace saw firsthand and for the first time in this incarnation the violet flame in action in the transmutation of the records of the past.

EXPERIENCE THE MARVELOUS ACTION OF THE VIOLET FIRE

Wherever you are, as you read my words you can begin to experience the marvelous action of the violet fire coursing through your veins, penetrating the layers of the physical temple—the bloodstream, the nervous system, the brain—pressing through the chakras, swirling through the etheric body, passing over the pages of the written record of your incarnations on earth. Line by line, letter by letter, the flame—intelligent, luminous, directed by the mind of God—sets free the energies, electron by electron, of all past misuses of the sacred fire. And thus not one jot or tittle of the law of karma shall pass until all be fulfilled in the freedom of the violet fire.

If you would have the benefit of this miraculous energy, if you would be visited by the genie of the lamp of freedom, the master Saint Germain himself, you have but to make the call. For the fiat of Almighty God has gone forth, and it is cosmic law: The call compels the answer! But the call is a very special call. It is not the demand of the human consciousness, but the command of your Real Self, your own true being, the mediator between the I AM Presence and the soul. Thus you declare:

> In the name of the Christ Self and in the name of the living God, I call forth the energies of the sacred fire from the altar within my heart. In the name of the I AM THAT I AM, I invoke the violet flame to blaze forth from

the center of the threefold flame, from the white-fire core of my own I AM Presence, multiplied by the momentum of the blessed ascended master Saint Germain. I call forth that light to penetrate my soul and to activate my soul memory of freedom and the original blueprint of my soul's destiny.

I call forth the violet transmuting flame to pass through my four lower bodies and through my soul consciousness to transmute the cause and core of all that is less than my Christ-perfection, all that is not in keeping with the will of God for my lifestream.

So let it be done by the cloven tongues of the fire of the Holy Spirit in fulfillment of the action of that sacred fire, as Above, so below. And I accept it done this hour in the full power of the living God who even now declares within my soul, "I AM WHO I AM."

As you begin to use the violet flame, you will experience feelings of joy, lightness, hope, and newness of life as though clouds of depression were being dissolved by the very sun of your own being. And the oppression of the very dark, dank energies of human bondage literally melts in the fervent heat of freedom's violet fires.

Let the energies of the violet flame unlock your True Self even as they sweep away the encrustations of the synthetic self. Let the violet flame work in you the works of God.

7

A HEART MEDITATION

As we contemplate the light of the violet flame, won't you go within the heart. Close your eyes and go into your heart. Look at your heart with your eyes closed. See first the white light. It is a torch of fire blazing. See it about three inches high in the center of your chest.

Visualize yourself in meditation invoking the Sun of your own being—that magnificent atom of Self. It is your energy. And every single moment of every day and night, you are deciding what to do with that energy.

Visualize the chest cavity as a brilliant sun. (Take a snapshot in your mind's eye of the sun at noonday when you look high in the heavens and you see that whirling ball of fire. It is a fiery sphere —so fiery and intense you cannot look upon it.

Now visualize that sun in your heart.) Enter this inner chamber and visualize yourself suspended in that sphere of consciousness.

Now feel yourself following the lines of your body—from the extremities to the heart. Feel yourself pulling with your eyes, with your consciousness. Pull up the feet, the ankles, the heels, up the calves, up the knees.

Feel yourself pulling energy as though you were stretching your muscles—but your muscles are not moving. These are the muscles of your mind dictating to your body where energy is in a given moment. This energy is moving—pulling to the heart, all flowing to the heart.

Feel the energy flowing from the tips of your fingers, up your arms, your elbows, up to your shoulders to your heart. Feel your energies flowing from your head and your mind—all centering into the heart so that the heart is the center of consciousness, of self-awareness.

As you are absorbed in this great fire, remember that God himself is centered in this fire. This is your source in this plane of matter. You must be centered in this place to begin your meditation.

This is a new kind of concentration. It is letting go of the concentration of the mind. The mind is in neutral. But all energy of consciousness that is beyond the mind, the soul, the body are flowing into the heart.

Now see the violet fire as a dot the size of the head of a pin in your heart. Let your mind's eye concentrate on that head of that pin. See it as the beginning—the vortex of the violet flame from the point of the head of the pin. Do not take your eye from that head of that pin.

As you meditate on it, you will see the violet flame burst from its center and begin to weave in a clockwise direction. Now use a worded formula to further unlock the light, energy and consciousness of the violet flame.

Prayers and affirmations spoken aloud are powerful. In ancient times it was known as the art of invocation. In our time, we have the science of the spoken Word used in decrees that are like spoken dynamic poetry—short and rhythmic.

Words change the material world. As God said,

"Let there be light and there was light." We can focus this light and become co-creators through the spoken Word.

As you say these verses aloud, let the words flow almost automatically as your entire concentration is on that pin.

Remain centered in your heart where you see the beginning of the vortex of the violet flame. While maintaining a strong visualization, repeat the words to reinforce the energy matrix—create with sound and rhythm.

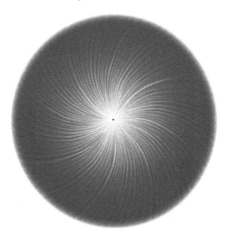

Radiant spiral violet flame,
   Descend, now blaze through me!
Radiant spiral violet flame,
   Set free, set free, set free!

Radiant violet flame, O come,
   Expand and blaze thy light through me!
Radiant violet flame, O come,
   Reveal God's power for all to see!
Radiant violet flame, O come,
   Awake the earth and set it free!

Radiance of the violet flame,
   Expand and blaze through me!
Radiance of the violet flame,
   Expand for all to see!
Radiance of the violet flame,
   Establish mercy's outpost here!
Radiance of the violet flame,
   Come, transmute now all fear!

8

VIOLET FLAME FOR PERSONAL AND WORLD KARMA

As our sponsor for the Aquarian age, Saint Germain wants to help us solve our karmic dilemmas so we can realize our highest potential. His solution: the violet flame. He says:

Karma is the weight that prevents the soul from flying. Karma affects all choices. It affects contracts—business, marriage and otherwise—those who are drawn to your life and those who cannot be, and the children you may give birth to.

Every day as percentages of karma pass through the violet flame and you ratify that transmutation by good deeds, words and works of love and service, you are lightening the load and therefore rising to new

planes of realization, new associations. . . .
The less karma you have, the greater your
opportunity day by day.[1]

Those of us who have regularly used the violet
flame in our prayers have watched it ease the burden and suffering of family and friends. It has
enhanced our creativity and helped us overcome
blocks to healing physical problems or emotional
hang-ups. It has helped us navigate through major
life challenges. It has helped us forgive others and
move beyond painful experiences.

With regular use, the violet flame can bring positive change into your life—and transmute the buildup
of mankind's karma that could result in the darkness
prophesied for our time. In short, the violet flame
affords us the optimum opportunity for self-transformation and world transformation. That is exactly
why Saint Germain, out of his great compassion for
our souls, gave us the gift of the violet flame.

The violet flame has long been used by spiritual
adepts. In the past it was also used by the people of
Atlantis when their golden-age civilization was at its
height. Because they eventually misused the violet

flame, in later centuries only the few were entrusted with its secrets. But in the early 1930s, Saint Germain reintroduced the violet flame to the world.

What great hope! What greatheartedness Saint Germain must have had that day when he literally unfurled the great ribbons of the violet flame that we have been blessed with ever since!

TRANSMUTING KARMA
AHEAD OF TIME

Today Saint Germain is sponsoring us to use the violet flame because he wants us to overcome the karmic challenges that loom on the horizon before they have a chance to weigh us down. For he knows that unless we invoke the violet flame to transmute our negative karma, sooner or later we will be compelled to balance it in other ways—ways that may severely restrict our options.

Saint Germain explains that the violet flame has the ability to change physical conditions because, of all the flames, the violet is closest in vibratory action to the components of matter. "The violet flame can combine with any molecule or molecular structure, any particle of matter known or unknown, and any wave of light, electron or electricity," he says. Wherever people gather together to give violet-flame prayers, "there you notice immediately an improvement in physical conditions."

The violet flame can literally consume the debris within and between the atoms of your being. It's like soaking them in a chemical solution that, layer by layer, dissolves the dirt that has been trapped there for thousands of years.

A major factor in energy flow is karma. Karma is the effect of causes we have set in motion in the past, whether ten minutes ago or ten embodiments ago. We have all grown up learning about karma. We just didn't call it that. Instead, we heard: *What goes around comes around. Whatsoever a man soweth, that shall he also reap. For every action there is an equal and opposite reaction. And in the end, the love you take is equal to the love you make.*

Every moment energy is flowing to us from God, and every moment we are deciding whether we will put a positive or negative spin on it. By the law of the circle, the law of karma, that energy will return to us. When the positive energy returns, we see positive things come into our life. The energy that has our negative stamp on it, because we have used that energy to harm rather than help others, also returns to its source—this time seeking resolution. It returns to us as opportunity to make things right.

When we don't transform that returning energy

into something positive, it doesn't just go away. It collects and then calcifies in our physical, mental or emotional worlds. As a result of this karmic clutter, we don't feel as light, free, happy, vibrant and spiritual as we could.

Negative energy can also build up on a large scale when groups of people contribute, for instance, to pollution, prejudice, persecution. When this "group karma" returns en masse, it can have large-scale consequences, such as the wars or earth changes that prophets have foreseen for our time. How we deal with our individual and group karma will determine whether these prophecies will come to pass.

THE KEY TO A NEW WORLD

Dannion Brinkley in his book *Saved by the Light* gives an eye-opening account of his near-death experiences. Like others who have had near-death experiences (NDEs), he tells of going through a tunnel and being escorted by a being of light. But unlike other NDEers, he remembers where he went and what he saw with much more detail.

During his first NDE, a being of light led

Dannion to a city of crystal cathedrals, which were really halls of learning. At one of these cathedrals, thirteen beings of light revealed to him events that would take place in the future. Of the 117 revelations he recalls, almost 100 have come to pass.

Dannion spoke about his life-changing experiences at a spiritual conference we held in July 1997. After that, he told me that during his near-death sojourns he saw the violet flame. "I have seen the violet flame and felt the violet flame," he said. "When you pass from this world to the next, you automatically become the flame. You connect to it. I have done it. When you pass through the violet flame, you are connected to a new dimension."

"Every crystal city," he added, "has the violet flame as well as all the spiritual flames. But the violet flame is the greatest of the flames. The violet flame is the purest place of love. It's what really empowers you."

Dannion went on to share with me what he has learned about the violet flame.

The violet flame is a light that serves all spiritual heritages, that gives respect and dignity to all things. It gives us a way to connect with each other. That flame is inside of us. The flame *is* us.

• A new world is coming. It will change every day. Yes, there will be some turbulent moments, but it's changing for the better. And the violet flame will come and it will grow, and you who work with that flame will be contributors to that new world.

If you have one thing that grows and glows brighter than anything else in the innermost part of your being—the violet flame—then no matter what transitions we go through in the coming years, you will have a quiet, peaceful place within.

9

AFFIRMATIONS AND DECREES

In this chapter, we offer specific prayers, affirmations and decrees to the violet flame that you can use to bring spiritual solutions to the prophesied challenges of our time. We have also included suggested visualizations and meditations that can enhance your spiritual practice and help you fulfill your unique purpose in life.

An effective exercise to start your day with is the "Heart, Head and Hand Decrees." This set of affirmations helps purify and energize heart, head and hand for a greater mind-heart-body connection.

The heart is the place where we commune with God. It is the center from which we send out our love to nourish mankind. Our head is the chalice where we receive the creative thoughts of God and our Higher Self. Our hands represent how we put our spirituality into practice. All three—heart, head and hand—are an integral part of our spirituality.

HEART, HEAD AND HAND

We begin with the heart because the heart is the hub of life, physically and spiritually. With the "Heart" mantra, we call forth the transmutative power of the violet flame. Layer by layer, the violet flame can dissolve negative feelings and karma that block the flow of energy through the heart. The "Heart" mantra helps us develop the qualities of the heart. It helps us become more open, more sensitive and more compassionate to the plight of so many who need our love and our prayers.

The "Head" mantra clears the physical and spiritual faculties of the mind so that we can think and communicate more clearly. It helps us strengthen our intuitive faculties and develop a keener perception to spiritual dimensions.

In the "Hand" mantra we affirm our partnership with Spirit and we say, "When I join hands with God, nothing will be impossible." The hand symbolizes the power of God to make things happen —through our profession, our service to life, the big and small things we do for others every day. Through our hand we can transfer tremendous energy and healing.

With the "Hand" mantra we also affirm that we will walk the "Middle Way," as Gautama Buddha taught his followers. After his own experimentation, Gautama said the best way to make spiritual progress is to live a balanced life, not succumbing to the extremes of asceticism or indulgence.

Visualization and Meditation:

As you recite the "Heart" mantra, visualize the violet flame within your heart as a pulsating violet light that softens your heart and allows the petals of your heart chakra to open. See the violet flame transforming anger into compassion, bitterness into sweetness, anxiety into peace.

As you give the "Head" mantra, see the violet flame leaping up from your heart and penetrating into your head to clear your mind of all mental blocks, negative images and limiting concepts about yourself or others. See your mind becoming filled with the brilliant light of God.

As you give the "Hand" mantra, visualize the

violet flame dissolving the cause, effect, record and memory of those things you had a "hand" in that you wish you had not done. You can give each section below three times, or as many times as you wish.

Heart

Violet fire, thou love divine,
Blaze within this heart of mine!
Thou art mercy forever true,
Keep me always in tune with you.

Head

I AM light, thou Christ in me,
Set my mind forever free;
Violet fire, forever shine
Deep within this mind of mine.

God who gives my daily bread,
With violet fire fill my head
Till thy radiance heavenlike
Makes my mind a mind of light.

Hand

I AM the hand of God in action,
Gaining victory every day;
My pure soul's great satisfaction
Is to walk the Middle Way.

THE WHITE LIGHT

The next set of affirmations reinforces our Protective "tube of light," shown in the Chart of Your Divine Self (page 84). The tube of light is a shield of protective white light about nine feet in diameter that streams down from God and the I AM THAT I AM above you and extends beneath your feet.

The tube of light can guard against energies of malice that may be directed at you through someone's anger, condemnation, hatred or jealousy. When you are unprotected, those vibrations can make you irritable or depressed. They can even cause you to have accidents.

The white light can also protect you from the pull of the mass consciousness. When we feel exhausted after a trip into the city or after we go shopping during the holiday rush, it's often because our light has been drained. The tube of light helps us stay centered and at peace.

It's a good idea to give your "Tube of Light" decree each morning before the hustle and bustle of the day begins. If throughout the day you feel deenergized, depleted or vulnerable, you can repeat this decree as needed. "The tube of light is invincible," says Saint Germain. "Reinforce it after you have been for a while midst many people and in the commercial world. Withdraw for a few minutes. Reestablish the fire!"

Visualization and Meditation:

As you recite the "Tube of Light" decree, see the dazzling white light from your I AM Presence, brighter than the sun shining on new-fallen snow, coalescing to form an impenetrable wall of light around you. Inside this scintillating tube of light, see yourself enfolded with the violet flame. From time to time throughout the day, you can reinforce this spiritual protection by visualizing the tube of light around you and repeating the decree.

Tube of Light

Beloved I AM Presence bright,
Round me seal your tube of light
From ascended master flame
Called forth now in God's own name.
Let it keep my temple free
From all discord sent to me.

I AM calling forth violet fire
To blaze and transmute all desire,
Keeping on in freedom's name
Till I AM one with the violet flame.

FORGIVENESS

The next decree is for forgiveness. The violet flame is a forgiving flame. Forgiveness is not always easy, but without forgiveness we cannot make spiritual progress. When we refuse to forgive a friend or a supposed enemy who has wronged us, even if he wrongs us again and again, we tie ourselves not only to that person but to his anger. Therefore, we are not truly free until we resolve the anger and balance the karma.

There may be times when we feel we cannot forgive someone because we believe the crime they committed against us or a loved one has been too great. In a situation like this, God has taught me that we should forgive the soul and ask God to bind the not-self of the person that caused him to commit the crime. No matter how bad a person's deeds are, we should always forgive the soul, thereby avoiding a karmic entanglement. Hatred binds; love frees.

Spiritually speaking, each time we don't forgive someone, we are putting a barrier between ourselves and another part of God. And sometimes the most important person you have to forgive is yourself.

Visualization and Meditation:

As you give the "Forgiveness" mantra, send your love and forgiveness to all whom you have ever wronged and all who have ever wronged you, releasing the situations into God's hands.

Forgiveness

I AM Forgiveness acting here,
Casting out all doubt and fear,

Setting men forever free
With wings of cosmic Victory.

I AM calling in full power
For Forgiveness every hour;
To all life in every place
I flood forth forgiving Grace.

THE LIGHT OF THE HEART

Many spiritual traditions tell us that the heart should be the centerpiece of our spirituality. Saint Germain has written a beautiful prayer called "I AM the Light of the Heart" to celebrate the divine flame within our hearts and to help us become heart-centered. He says:

Your heart is indeed one of the choicest gifts of God. Within it there is a central chamber surrounded by such light and protection as that which we call a "cosmic interval." It is a chamber separated from matter, and no probing could ever discover it.

It occupies simultaneously not only the third and fourth dimensions but also other dimensions unknown to man. It is thus the connecting point of the mighty silver cord of light that descends from your divine God Presence to sustain the beating of your physical heart, giving you life, purpose and cosmic integration.

I urge all to treasure this point of contact that they have with life by paying conscious recognition to it. You do not need to understand by sophisticated language or scientific postulation the how, why and wherefore of this activity.

Be content to know that God is there and that there is within you a point of contact with the Divine, a spark of fire from the Creator's own heart which is called the threefold flame of life. There it burns as the triune essence of love, wisdom and power.

Each acknowledgment paid daily to the flame within your heart will amplify the power and illumination of love within your being. Each such attention will produce a new sense of dimension for you, if not outwardly apparent then subconsciously manifest within the folds of your inner thoughts.

Neglect not, then, your heart as the altar of God. Neglect it not as the sun of your manifest being. Draw from God the power of love and amplify it within your heart. Then send it out into the world at large as the bulwark of that which shall overcome the darkness of the planet. . . .

Remember that as long as you face the light, the shadows are always behind. And the light is there, too, to transmute them all.[1]

Visualization and Meditation:

As you recite "I AM the Light of the Heart," visualize light descending from your I AM Presence and Holy Christ Self to your heart, where it will be released according to the worded matrix of your decree.

Then center your attention on your heart. Picture the brilliance of the sun at noonday and transfer that picture to the center of your chest, where your heart chakra is located.

Now see thousands of sunbeams going forth from your heart to penetrate and dissolve any darkness, despair or depression first within yourself and then within the people of the world.

Project your love (which is really God's love) out into the world. See that love as intense fiery-pink laser beams that break down all barriers to the success of your relationships, your family, your spiritual growth, your career, your neighborhood or your nation.

I AM the Light of the Heart

I AM the Light of the Heart
Shining in the darkness of being
And changing all into the golden treasury
Of the Mind of Christ.

I AM projecting my Love
Out into the world
To erase all errors
And to break down all barriers.

I AM the power of infinite Love,
Amplifying itself
Until it is victorious,
World without end!

"I AM THE VIOLET FLAME"

"I AM the Violet Flame" is a powerful decree that you can repeat many times to build a strong action of transmutation.

Visualization and Meditation:

See the violet flame come to life as if you were looking at a movie. The flames rise and pulsate around you in different shades and gradations of purple, pink and violet.

See these flames pass through your body, caressing each organ and restoring wholeness. See them saturating your mind and your emotions, relieving all burdens.

One of my favorite visualizations for this decree is to see the seven seas filled with violet flame. Meditate on the power of the seven seas and then translate that image into a giant, peaceful violet-flame sea that envelops the entire planet. Imagine the weight of it, the power of it, the energy of it. The violet flame has the capacity to totally transform the earth, the air and the waters.

You can apply this decree to specific situations.

You can see the violet flame transmuting the pollution in a local river or clearing the smog over your city. You can focus on the world's children. Visualize them before you, starting with the children of your own neighborhood and moving on to the needy children of the world. See frolicking, dancing violet flames swaddling them and transforming their burdens into joy.

I AM the Violet Flame

I AM the violet flame
    In action in me now
I AM the violet flame
    To Light alone I bow
I AM the violet flame
    In mighty cosmic power
I AM the light of God
    Shining every hour
I AM the violet flame
    Blazing like a sun
I AM God's sacred power
    Freeing every one.

10

THE GREAT MYSTERY OF THE VIOLET FLAME

by a Master of the Violet Flame

Let us speak of the mastery of the violet flame since you are familiar with it and it does not strike a certain fear, as the physical flames of earth's fire sometimes do. Therefore, beloved, be seated in the violet flame. . . .

Visualization of the violet flame begins your concentration and results in your God-mastery. Visualize the fire in the heart, then, and let the violet flame burn in the heart, surround the heart. . . .

And when you know your mantras by heart, as many of you do, then sit in deep meditation and let the violet flame increase in size, beginning within and then encompassing the physical heart and the heart chakra. Let the action of the violet flame remain intense by your visualization and by the intensity of your call. Then let it expand slowly so that the intensity is such that you cannot see through the flame; for it has become a dense manifestation of the violet ray of light as it has descended from the sun and then sprung up as a flame at your point of invocation. . . .

THE MYSTERY OF THE MANTRA

Your point of invocation is your throat chakra. It can also be defined as the plane of your soul's incarnation. Therefore I say, invoke the flame through the throat chakra and add to your invocation the instrument of the heart chakra, thereby pouring love to the flame and drawing love from the flame. Use the third eye to invoke the violet flame by intense visualization, drawing the flame into the third eye and giving to the flame the momentum of the sacred fire of that chakra. So use each of the chakras to meditate upon the flame, to focus the flame and then to give devotion unto the flame even as you receive the devotion of the flame. . . .

The more creative you are in the use of the

violet flame, the more you understand that the violet flame is a ritual, has a consciousness of ritual and looks forward to the hours of the day that you have consecrated to invoking a mantra of the violet flame—or, should I say, invoking the violet flame through a mantra?

Well, the mantra is the flame and the flame is God and so is the mantra! The question is: Are you all three? Are you the flame, the mantra and the manifestation of God?

This is the attainment you look forward to as you visualize the violet flame rising up from beneath your feet, rising and pulsating and purifying every level of your being. Then when the concentration is complete in the physical body and you see and feel it, let it slowly extend out from you as an aura having the magnetism of the violet flame and let it increase and intensify.

And so, beloved, as you go through the world, remember to put on your tube of light to protect your momentum of the violet flame. But also be ready when you see the eyes of a lightbearer and the child in need and the soul who looks to God for help. Do not fear to be the instrument to transfer a cup of cool violet flame in Christ's name. . . .

In no other past age since the last age of Aquarius, twelve cycles ago, has there been such an opportunity for world transmutation, soul transmutation, the balancing of karma and your soul's restoration through the Lord and Saviour Jesus Christ to your own inner Christ-potential. So, beloved, the opportunity is vast.

Why, all the retreats of the entire planet are simply pulsating with the joy of the violet flame!

So you see, beloved, you can do the same! You can bank the fires of the violet flame in all of your chakras and in all of the levels of your being, as tier upon tier your chakras represent the seven planes of heaven. You can rise up those tiers, beloved ones!

THE VIOLET FLAME
IN THE SEVEN CHAKRAS

Now understand, beloved, the great mystery of the violet flame. The violet flame is an action that can be stepped up or down and tuned to any level of the seven chakras. Therefore the violet flame that you keep in the heart will have a different frequency than the violet flame that you keep in the solar-plexus chakra, and so on. And as you are stepping up the grades of the violet flame from the base-of-the-spine chakra to the crown chakra, there is an acceleration of the violet flame affecting all of those levels in the earth body. So when you begin at the base chakra and proceed, rising to the crown, you are experiencing God in the seven levels of heaven right in your very own being!

Therefore I say to you, value the chakras in your body. Value them well, beloved, for they are chalices. And in the day and the hour when sudden calamity or terminal disease or plague of any kind comes upon your house or upon your body, you will have vials filled with violet flame as a precious medicine, as a precious unguent that you may use spiritually and physically.

For where there are pockets of concentration of the violet flame and you in your joy and love for beloved Saint Germain and Portia and all they have ever done for you do keep that violet flame, well, you see, you are as points igniting a whole world with the violet flame. You are practically as a tinderbox! And someone may come along and invoke a single violet flame and catch the whole momentum that you carry. And therefore the violet flame will be contagious! And it will leap from heart to heart, from continent to continent, from village to village!

Do you understand, beloved? Our goal is to see planet Earth become, as she should be, a Violet Planet herself!

THE VIOLET FLAME
AND THE SEVEN RAYS

Happy are ye when ye have illumination! You may think I have brought to you the violet flame, but I have brought to you the violet flame of illumination's flame!

Now hear this. There is the violet flame of the blue ray. There is the violet flame of the yellow ray. There is the violet flame of the pink ray. There is the violet flame of the white ray. There is the violet flame of the green ray. There is the violet flame of the purple and gold ray flecked with ruby. And there is the violet flame of the seventh ray of the violet flame!

Now therefore, beloved, see how the violet flame can clarify in the mind, the heart, the body and the being all of the understanding, all of the knowledge, all of the perception, all of the senses, all of the functions of the chakras. This can happen when they are cleansed and revivified and purified by the elixir of the violet flame. Why, you see every color more brilliantly! You see the crystal and the white-fire core of each ray more brilliantly!

So the violet flame has an aspect on each of the seven rays. And as you invoke it and allow it to complement the seven rays, beloved ones, you will learn more about those rays than you have ever learned by just concentrating upon those rays alone.

SET THE WORLD ON FIRE

The violet flame is surely the universal aura of the planet in this hour, for many angels and elementals and Keepers of the Flame have invoked it. I say, continue to invoke it! For the greatest miracles of all will come to you through this flame and through this flame combined with others.

I bring to you—and all of the priesthood of Melchizedek who are here with me this night bring to you—candles, candles of the violet flame. The wax, or substance like it, is of the violet-flame color and the flame is the violet-flame color.

Now take your candle, beloved ones. Hold it before you! Be at peace! *Be* a Keeper of the Flame! *And go set the world on fire with violet flame!*

11

THE DOORWAY TO INFINITY

by Saint Germain

I know that the desire is upon your heart to know and understand what God has appointed you to do in this life and in previous lifetimes. I know that you have a deep desiring to fulfill all things so that you might arrive at the gate of the next world having fully accomplished your mission.

I can assure you that the violet flame will assist you in accelerating both that mission and those spirals of light that are in every atom and cell of your being. I assure you that you can encapsulate time and accelerate time and that you will find yourself accomplishing in ten years what without the violet flame could take you a century.

The violet flame does shorten the distance.

It does increase the capacity of every moment and hour. It accelerates the functioning of the mind and the ability of the body to be rejuvenated.

If you look for the elixir of eternal youth, I tell you it is the violet flame. Drink of it daily! If you look for the regeneration of certain parts of the body, if you look for the revitalizing of the mind and heart and even for the spiral of the resurrection flame to enfold your entire being, invoke the power, wisdom, love of the Trinity and call forth showers upon showers upon showers of living violet flame of the seventh ray.

Know and discover, then, the alchemy of the Spirit. Do not lament lost hours or years or days but know that from this moment of the eternal Now, you can live in eternity while yet walking the earth in these forms you yet wear. You can be renewed each day and you can walk that perfect path because of the violet flame.[1]

Children of the Sun, ye are of an ancient memory and one with the forces of light. Ten thousand years and more you have awaited this hour of your coming and mine for the fervent release of the seventh ray to an age beset with the accumulation of the karma not alone of two thousand years but many....

Indeed, it is possible for you to transcend all of the cycles of your karma in this age. But whatever the calling or the choosing of your soul, remember it cannot be accomplished without the Holy Spirit's gift to you of the violet flame. And truly it is given in this hour. And there is no mantra more necessary to your deliverance and survival—for the violet flame is a physical flame!

And, beloved, it is the physical atoms of the earth that are burdened with disease and death and toxins and chemical pollutants that burden the body and prevent the mind from being the chalice of the diamond-shining mind of God, which is your rightful inheritance from the universal Christ....

Therefore, my beloved—those who have known me forever, those who only recently have made my acquaintance—I tell you that I took the name Saint Germain, for it means "holy brother." May you think of me always as your friend and brother on the Path. And may you know that I may not enter your world to intercede for you unless you call my name in the name of God and ask.

Therefore, say it to me any hour of the day or night—"In the name of Almighty God, Saint Germain, help me now!" I promise you that an Electronic Presence of myself shall be at your side with the speed of light.

And if you desire to increase your capacity to receive my assistance, then take up the calls to the violet flame and see how your aura will actually turn a violet color so that friends may see it and feel the impact of the seventh ray.

When your aura is so charged, beloved, I may then enter it and repolarize your very physical form to the light of God that never fails, to the inner blueprint and the image of Christ in which ye are made!

From the beginning unto the ending, I AM Saint Germain, one with the Keepers of the Flame worldwide. O beloved, let me help you! Receive me now as your friend forever.[2]

The violet flame does etch in fire and crystal the image of the divine man that ye are! It is not alone for transmutation of karma. The violet flame is that which seals the creation in the glory of God in the seventh day and the Sabbath rest, when all that you have ever brought forth in all aeons is now sifted by the violet flame.

And the jewels and the nuggets, the virtues, the inventions, the music of the spheres that you have brought forth—all these are immortalized together with your own soul by the violet transmuting flame. And the rest that is not worth keeping is consumed under the studious ministration of angels of the seventh ray....

Blessed ones, what you can do to work planetary change is unlimited. I said it is unlimited! The infinite power of God *is* available to you, greater than all nuclear power or weapons. This is not a theory or a metaphysical statement. It is a law that you can make physical by the spiritual fire merging in the chalice of being.[3]

I desire that you should understand the great equation of the century, that by an acceleration of dynamic decrees of the violet flame and loving service to life you may balance an extraordinary percentage of your karma; and if you reach that level of 51 percent, beloved, you will not be required to reincarnate, come what may upon this planet.

This is a great boon of dispensation from the LORD God, and thereby many have achieved that point of permanency and well-being—peace in the profound recesses of the temple of being—and thus a fearlessness that comes of a fire that intensifies.[4]

Some of you have come to me for many years in wonder and consternation that you make not further progress on the Path. And somehow you have overlooked the universal solvent of the violet flame.

You have found, then, the alchemist's dream in this violet fire. Use it. Use it as the Elohim themselves scheme to bring forth the perfect man and the Manchild. Use the violet flame to go beyond yourself, to exceed yourself. It is the law of self-transcendence. See what it can do.

Beloved hearts, never, never do we desire to hear it spoken, "It might have been." What might have been is that which is past and cannot be recalled. Therefore let us dwell on what is. And let us visualize the violet flame at the nexus of the hourglass. And therefore it transmutes time and Father Time and the cycles of time running out. It transmutes space. And at that point of the nexus, . . . realize the precipitation of infinity.

Thus there is expansion of opportunity, which means expansion of cycles, which means transcending of time and space so that you are no longer bound by laws of mortality or limitation and therefore can, in the given life span, accomplish all that you desire, all that the Law requires. And this expansion of your days, this increasing of your days with joy has to do with the capacity of atoms, cells, and electrons and chakras and forcefields in your being that you know not of—the increase of the capacity to hold light.

It is ever our desire that you should come into a scientific understanding of how to increase that capacity. Let us begin with a visualization of the violet flame at the nexus. . . . "Time is not. Space is no more." Thus in this sense of infinity, you have indeed eternal life here and now.[5]

- 12 -

THE ALCHEMY OF LOVE

We have been talking about the mind-body connection in using the violet flame, but the scientific power of prayer is really a mind-*heart*-body connection.

Prayer should not be just a mental exercise or the performance of a rote ritual. The fire of your heart and your love is what compels the angels to answer your calls. Love is what gives shape to our desires and what should guide our visualizations. So the more heartfelt our prayers are, the more charged they are with spiritual purpose.

Saint Germain talks about this mind-heart-body connection and how the violet flame has been able to help many at deep levels to make both inner and outer progress. In these excerpts, he describes how it has softened the heart and helped heal old hurts.

The violet flame turns around the downward spiral of the chakras and the negative energy.... The violet flame is the buoyant joy...that turns around spirits and minds and souls and emotions![1]

Blessed ones, first and foremost the greatest good has come to the individual supplicant himself. Therefore, to those who have so loved this ritual, there has been an increase of transmutation. And I have seen to it, as you count me as your master and friend, that that violet flame which you have invoked has been directed into the most resistant and recalcitrant pockets of your own subconscious, especially into those conditions that you have been the most desirous to have removed.

Therefore, in some of you a hearty amount of karma has been balanced, in others hardness of heart has truly melted around the heart chakra. There has come a new love and a new softening, a new compassion, a new sensitivity to life.....

The violet flame has assisted in relationships within families. It has served to liberate some to balance old karmas and old hurts and to set individuals on their courses according to their vibration. . . .

It is impossible to enumerate exhaustively all of the benefits of the violet flame, but there is indeed an alchemy that does take place within the personality. The violet flame goes after the schisms that cause psychological problems that go back to early childhood and previous incarnations and that have established such deep grooves within the consciousness that in fact they have been difficult to shake lifetime after lifetime. . . .

The violet flame is a considerate flame. It is a loving flame. . . . It may be difficult to understand how a flame can have consciousness, but remember, a flame is the manifestation of God. A flame is the manifestation of all who have ever served it, even as a mantra embodies the momentum of all who have ever given it. . . .

Blessed ones, I can only say that if you could see what inner progress you have made, you would not cease in the giving of those violet-flame recordings as often as possible—not necessarily all at once, but if you make the effort, you can endow those segments of time that come to you in the day with your decree momentum on that flame. And therefore, as you should come to understand, whatever time of day you invoke a flame or perform a service it does tie into your karma made at that very same hour throughout history. . . .

In the etheric retreats where you study [as your soul travels out of the body at night], you are shown the filigree thread of light that emits from a heart chakra filled with mercy's love. Some of you have seen where there have been a number of threads so great as to not even be possible of counting, and these threads of violet flame, almost as a gossamer veil, have gone directly to hearts all over the planet.

You have observed these threads, almost as fine as hair, being as vessels, even as veins within the body, carrying a continual flow of violet flame that has enabled individuals all over the world to rise up, to accomplish things they have not accomplished in many lifetimes, to experience hope and healing and a new desire to find God, to be free and to stand for the cause of freedom. . . .

You can in fifteen minutes a day [of giving violet-flame decrees] have me with you; and in my presence with you, you can deliver a momentum of violet flame to many souls upon the planet.[2]

———————————

I invite you to experiment with the violet-flame decrees and see what happens. It is my prayer that the sweet people of the world will come together with open hearts and, with a spirit of joy and a vision of hope, give violet-flame decrees. I, for one, would do this simply out of gratitude to Saint Germain, who has continued to work with our souls at great personal sacrifice for thousands of years.

The future is truly in our hands. Our choices now and in the next years will make all the difference for generations to come.

NOTES

CHAPTER 1 • **Saint Germain:**
            Alchemist, Adept and Visionary

1. See Godfré Ray King, *Unveiled Mysteries,* 3rd ed. (Chicago: Saint Germain Press, 1939), pp. 39–61.

2. Isa. 11:1.

3. Thomas Whittaker, *The Neo-Platonists: A Study in the History of Hellenism,* 2nd ed. (Cambridge: Cambridge University Press, 1928), p. 165.

4. Victor Cousin and Thomas Taylor, trans., *Two Treatises of Proclus, The Platonic Successor* (London: n.p., 1833), p. vi.

5. Geoffrey of Monmouth, *Vita Merlini,* in Nikolai Tolstoy, *The Quest for Merlin* (Boston: Little, Brown & Co., 1985), p. 217.

6. Brendan LeHane et al., *The Enchanted World: Wizards and Witches* (Chicago: Time Life Books, 1984), p. 34.

7. Sir Thomas Malory understood that King Arthur had at least two sisters. One Margawse married King Loth and bore him four sons, the oldest of whom was Gawain. She or another sister, alleges Malory, bore Modred to King Arthur. (Norma Lorre Goodrich, *King Arthur* [New York: Franklin Watts, 1986], p. 221.)

8. Henry Thomas and Dana Lee Thomas, *Living Biographies of Great Scientists* (Garden City, N.Y.: Nelson Doubleday, 1941), p. 15.

9. Ibid., p. 16.

10. Ibid., p. 17; David Wallechinsky, Amy Wallace, and Irving Wallace, *The Book of Predictions* (New York: William Morrow and Co., 1980), p. 346.

11. Thomas, *Living Biographies,* p. 20.

12. Wallechinsky and Wallace, *Book of Predictions,* p. 346.

13. Clements R. Markham, *Life of Christopher Columbus* (London: George Philip & Son, 1892), pp. 207–8.

14. Isa. 11:11, 12.

15. *Encyclopaedia Britannica,* 15th ed., s.v. "Columbus, Christopher."

16. Francis Bacon's word-cipher was discovered by cryptographer Dr. Orville W. Owen, who published five volumes of *Sir Francis Bacon's Cipher Story* between 1893 and 1895. The story hidden in his word-cipher can be constructed by stringing together words, lines, and passages from the works of various Elizabethan writers. In contrast, deciphering the bi-literal cipher is an exact, scientific process of grouping together the italic letters (printed in two different fonts of type) that appear with peculiar frequency in original editions of the Shakespearean plays and other of Bacon's works. This cipher was discovered by an assistant of Dr. Owen, Mrs. Elizabeth Wells Gallup, who first published the stories Bacon had

concealed in his bi-literal cipher in 1899. To insure that his ciphers would eventually be discovered and his true life story revealed, Bacon had described in detail the bi-literal method of cipher writing in his Latin version of *De Augmentis* (1624), which some 270 years later Mrs. Gallup studied and applied. Ironically, Mrs. Gallup found that Bacon's bi-literal cipher contained complete directions on how to construct the word-cipher, which was actually discovered first by Dr. Owen.

17. Will Durant, *The Story of Philosophy: The Lives and Opinions of the Greater Philosophers* (Garden City, N.Y.: Garden City Publishing Co., 1927), p. 157.

18. The information detailed in the following paragraphs is taken from Margaret Barsi Greene, comp., *I, Prince Tudor, Wrote Shakespeare* (Boston: Branden Press, 1973), pp. 56–75, and Alfred Dodd, *The Martyrdom of Francis Bacon* (New York: Rider & Co., n.d.), p. 25.

19. Barsi Greene, *I, Prince Tudor,* p. 217.

20. Ibid., pp. 219–20.

21. Pallas Athena was often depicted wearing a helmet and full armor in her defense of truth. The traditions of ancient Greece depict her standing atop her majestic temple, holding a golden spear which, when glinted upon by the dawning sun, appeared to tremble. She is therefore known as the "shaker of the spear."

22. Saint Germain, November 4, 1966.

23. Barsi Greene, *I, Prince Tudor,* pp. 239, 243.

24. Saint Germain, October 14, 1991.

25. Saint Germain, September 3, 1973.

CHAPTER 2 • **A Sacred Fire**

1. Saint Germain, *Pearls of Wisdom,* vol. 15, no. 26.

CHAPTER 5 • **The Power of Sound**

1. In the past, individuals were required to balance 100 percent of their karma while still in embodiment in order to make their ascension. Under the dispensation of the Aquarian age, individuals may ascend after balancing 51 percent of their karma and can balance the remaining 49 percent from the heaven-world. For more on the process of the ascension, see Annice Booth, *The Path to Your Ascension: Rediscovering Life's Ultimate Purpose* (Gardiner, Mont.: Summit University Press, 1999).

CHAPTER 8 • **Violet Flame for Personal and World Karma**

1. Saint Germain, April 16, 1988.

CHAPTER 9 • **Affirmations and Decrees**

1. Saint Germain, February 12, 1967.

CHAPTER 10 • **The Great Mystery of the Violet Flame**

This chapter is excerpted from *Pearls of Wisdom,* vol. 35, no. 37.

CHAPTER 11 • **The Doorway to Infinity**

1. Saint Germain, *Pearls of Wisdom,* vol. 34, no. 64.
2. Saint Germain, *Pearls of Wisdom,* vol. 30, no. 6.
3. Saint Germain, *Pearls of Wisdom,* vol. 30, no. 10.
4. Saint Germain, *Pearls of Wisdom,* vol. 31, no. 50.
5. Saint Germain, *Pearls of Wisdom,* vol. 23, no. 32.

CHAPTER 12 • **The Alchemy of Love**

1. Saint Germain, December 2, 1984.
2. Saint Germain, July 4, 1988.

RESOURCES FOR YOUR VIOLET-FLAME EXPERIENCE

VioletFlame.com

Explore the violet flame with videos, meditations, and articles. Plus sign up for the Violet Flame Challenge and receive thirty days of emails to support your violet-flame spiritual practice.

AscendedMastersSpiritualRetreats.org

Explore the beautiful world of the ascended masters' etheric retreats. Hear vivid descriptions of different retreats on the site's *Touring Heaven* podcast.

YouTube Channel

Enjoy violet-flame mantras and Elizabeth Clare Prophet's in-depth teaching on the violet flame: www.SummitLighthouse.org/VioletFlameVideos

Resources at The Summit Lighthouse

Our website has many articles on the violet flame and techniques on how to apply it to different challenges and circumstances of life:

www.SummitLighthouse.org/violet-flame/

Visualizations for the
Heart, Head and Hand Decrees

www.SummitLighthouse.org/HHH-Decrees

Keepers of the Flame Fraternity

Visit KeepersOfTheFlame.org to find out how you can join a spiritual fraternity sponsored by Saint Germain. Includes access to confidential teachings from Saint Germain and other ascended masters through 33 lessons.

540 pp • ISBN 978-0-916766-68-9

Saint Germain On Alchemy

Formulas for Self-Transformation

"If you think alchemy is just some archaic sleight of hand for changing lead into gold, Saint Germain On Alchemy will set you straight. It's about transformation: transforming yourself— first spiritually and then materially. But it doesn't stop there. Alchemy aims to transform the world itself, to guide the unfold-ment of history." —Richard Nolle, author of *Critical Astrology*

Four books in one, including *Studies in Alchemy* and *Intermediate Studies in Alchemy* plus a section on how to experience the full potential of your heart.

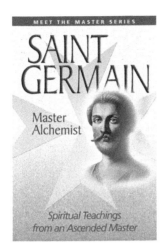

160 pp • ISBN 978-0-922729-95-1

Saint Germain
Master Alchemist

Spiritual Teachings from an Ascended Master

In the 1700s he dazzled royal courts and became known as the
Wonderman of Europe. Throughout history, the master Saint
Germain has played many key roles. Today he is the immortal
sponsor of the Aquarian age. Includes his priceless alchemical
secrets for personal transformation.

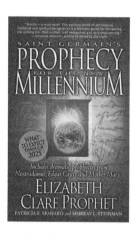

396 pp • ISBN 978-0-922729-45-6

Saint Germain's Prophecy for the New Millennium

Includes Dramatic Prophecies from Nostradamus, Edgar Cayce and Mother Mary

"Terrific—a must-read! This exciting blend of astrological, historical and spiritual perspectives is a fantastic guide for navigating the coming era. Well written, well researched and very empowering." —Dannion Brinkley, author of *Saved by the Light*

This timely work explores many of the most compelling prophecies for our time, including new interpretations of the celebrated quatrains of Nostradamus. Then it introduces us to a high-frequency spiritual energy that can bring balance, harmony and positive change into our lives. The dramatic insights and spiritual techniques revealed in this book will show you how to shape the future you want.

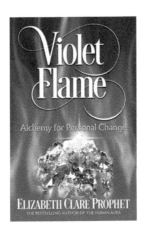

256 pp • ISBN 978-1-60988-274-7

Violet Flame

Alchemy for Personal Change

Learn how to use a high-frequency spiritual energy to transform your life and the world around you!

Mystical traditions East and West embrace the concept of a spiritual fire. Elizabeth Clare Prophet's book on the violet flame will show that sound, in the form of mantras, prayers, decrees and affirmations, can be used to call forth a spiritual fire known as the violet flame to transform every aspect of our lives and change our spiritual destinies.

Mrs. Prophet shares how we can harness the power of the violet flame by applying practical spiritual techniques to help restore health, balance, harmony as well as aide in creating positive and lasting changes to our personal lives, the lives of our loved ones and to the world around us.

112 pp • ISBN 978-0-922729-37-1

Violet Flame

To Heal Body, Mind and Soul

"The violet flame is a light that serves all spiritual heritages, that gives respect and dignity to all things. It gives us a way to connect with each other.... It's what really empowers you."
—Dannion Brinkley, author of *Saved by the Light*

Twentieth-century seer Edgar Cayce recognized the healing power of the violet light. Dannion Brinkley saw and experienced the violet flame in his near-death sojourns. Healers and alchemists have used this high-frequency spiritual energy to bring about energetic balance and spiritual transformation. Now you can learn how to apply the practical techniques in this book to create balance, harmony and positive change in body, mind and soul.

ABOUT
THE SUMMIT LIGHTHOUSE

Are you interested in the exploration of reality, pursuing individual self-mastery, and finding those points that are in common with the mystical paths of the world's religions?

The Summit Lighthouse, an endeavor of the great Brotherhood of light, is an international community of spiritual students who share your interest. We publish the teachings of the ascended masters in more than thirty languages and study them to accelerate on our spiritual path.

What are these teachings? Over the last 150 years, the ascended masters have again brought to mankind's attention the spiritual concepts of the ascension, karma and reincarnation, how to balance one's karma with the violet flame, finding one's twin flame and soul mates to accelerate fulfilling one's divine plan, soul liberation through the power of the spoken Word, prayer and meditation, and finding your point of identity with the reality of your I AM Presence—the divine spark within. They have also revealed the existence of the long-rumored Brotherhood of light that appears in times of need to help mankind.

What is this Brotherhood of light? It is comprised of men and women who mastered the fire of the heart, balanced their karma, fulfilled their dharma, and finally ascended into the light of the Presence of God. They return to help souls like you and me, their friends in past lives, to move beyond the limited self and into that Being that we really are.

The Summit Lighthouse has its international headquarters at the Royal Teton Ranch, a beautiful land in the Rocky Mountains just north of Yellowstone National Park. If you are in the area, we welcome you to drop by for a chat and enjoy our new Yellowstone Hot Springs! This beautiful mineral-rich hot spring is located in a spectacular setting on the banks of the Yellowstone River.

From anywhere in the world, you can explore our free online lessons on karma, chakras, the archangels, and an astounding story of Sanat Kumara, the Ancient of Days. Also check out our free book offer and sign up for our free series of sixteen *Pearls of Wisdom* on *The Chela and the Path* at: www. SummitLighthouse.org

While you're there, learn more about the teachings of the ascended masters, our spiritual community at the Royal Teton Ranch, weekend seminars, quarterly conferences, summer retreats, weekly *Pearls of Wisdom* from the ascended masters, the Keepers of the Flame Fraternity, and the study center nearest you.

For a free catalog of books, CDs, and DVDs published by Summit University Press, go to:

store.SummitLighthouse.org/summit-university-press-catalog-pdf-download

The Summit Lighthouse®
63 Summit Way, Gardiner, Montana
59030 USA

Se habla español.

TSLinfo@TSL.org
SummitLighthouse.org
www.ElizabethClareProphet.com
1-800-245-5445 / 406-848-9500

ELIZABETH CLARE PROPHET is a world-renowned author, spiritual teacher, and pioneer in practical spirituality. Her groundbreaking books have been published in more than thirty languages and over three million copies have been sold worldwide.

Among her best-selling titles are *The Human Aura; The Science of the Spoken Word; Your Seven Energy Centers; The Lost Years of Jesus; The Art of Practical Spirituality;* and her best-selling Pocket Guides to Practical Spirituality series.